# Emotional Sensitivity and Intensity

Teach®
Yourself

# Emotional Sensitivity and Intensity

How to manage emotions as a sensitive person

Imi Lo

First published in Great Britain in 2018 by Hodder & Stoughton.
An Hachette UK company.

Copyright © Imi Lo 2018

The right of Imi Lo to be identified as the Author of the Work has been asserted by her in accordance with the Copyright, Designs and Patents Act 1988.

Database right Hodder & Stoughton (makers)

The *Teach Yourself* name is a registered trademark of Hachette UK.

*British Library Cataloguing in Publication Data*: a catalogue record for this title is available from the British Library.

*Library of Congress Catalog Card Number*: on file.

ISBN 978 1 4736 5603 1

eISBN 978 1 4736 5604 8

4

The publisher has used its best endeavours to ensure that any website addresses referred to in this book are correct and active at the time of going to press. However, the publisher and the author have no responsibility for the websites and can make no guarantee that a site will remain live or that the content will remain relevant, decent or appropriate.

The publisher has made every effort to mark as such all words which it believes to be trademarks. The publisher should also like to make it clear that the presence of a word in the book, whether marked or unmarked, in no way affects its legal status as a trademark.

Every reasonable effort has been made by the publisher to trace the copyright holders of material in this book. Any errors or omissions should be notified in writing to the publisher, who will endeavour to rectify the situation for any reprints and future editions.

This book is for information or educational purposes only and is not intended to act as a substitute for medical advice or treatment. Any person with a condition requiring medical attention should consult a qualified medical practitioner or suitable therapist.

Typeset by Cenveo Publisher Services.

Printed and bound in Great Britain by CPI Group (UK) Ltd., Croydon, CR0 4YY.

John Murray Learning policy is to use papers that are natural, renewable and recyclable products and made from wood grown in sustainable forests. The logging and manufacturing processes are expected to conform to the environmental regulations of the country of origin.

Carmelite House

50 Victoria Embankment

London EC4Y 0DZ

www.hodder.co.uk

# Contents

# Introduction

Some people feel more than others.

If you are one of these people, then you experience emotions to a high level of depth and intensity. You soar high into bliss and plunge low into gloom, in rapid succession. You know the meaning of despair, as well as of beauty and rapture. As a perceptive observer of subtleties, you see, feel, notice and remember a lot. Your brain processes pieces of information and reflects on them with such speed and complexity that sometimes your words cannot keep up with your mind. You have an innate ability to feel into other people's energy. When it comes to relationships, you are naturally intuitive, loving, idealistic and romantic. You are always looking for more meaning in life, and feel a constant need to move forward. You might have been told that you are 'too much', 'too intense', 'too sensitive', 'too emotional', and that your behaviours are either 'too dramatic' or 'too timid'.

In recent years, growing awareness of emotional sensitivity and intensity has generated much interest, yet psychologists have so far been unable to agree on a definition. Some suggest that you are one of the 15–20 per cent of population who are wired differently as a highly sensitive person (HSP). Others call you an empath, a psychic, or simply someone with a 'thin skin'. At worst, you might be mislabelled as having a mental illness such as borderline personality disorder (BPD), bipolar disorder, ADHD or depression.

In this book, the phrases 'emotional sensitivity', 'emotional intensity' and 'emotional giftedness' are used interchangeably. This trait in itself is not a condition, but a strength that is often misunderstood in our culture. Many emotionally sensitive and intense people have an extraordinary capacity to understand the intentions, motivations and desires of other people, as well as the ability to reflect on their own feelings, fears and motivations. Their intensity is often paired with other forms of exceptional ability in the areas of music, visual art, logical thinking, body-awareness and sports. As you shall see in later chapters, emotional sensitivity is not only closely related to giftedness, it is a gift in itself.

However, emotionally intense people also face a unique set of interpersonal challenges. Since the ability to feel deeply and intensely often starts from a young age, when emotion regulation skills are lacking, you may have suffered psychological damage associated with rejection, shame and loneliness. As a gifted child, you were either over- or under-stimulated, or held back by social and cultural 'appropriateness'. You might have been troubled by feelings of inadequacy, guilt, a sense of responsibility for issues that were beyond your control, or you were accused of 'overreacting' or being 'too sensitive and dramatic'.

As an adult, you may be plagued with self-doubt, and a lingering sense of existential loneliness. On one hand you have to manage the hostility and judgements directed at you, while on the other hand you have to set appropriate boundaries for those who would like to benefit from your perceptive and intuitive abilities.

People born emotionally intense, sensitive and gifted are like the owners of powerful sports cars. These cars have extremely powerful engines that require a special fuel and a specific kind of care. In the right condition and with the right care, they can be one of the most high-performing machines in the world and win many races. The problem is, however, that their owners may not have been taught how to run these powerful vehicles.

In this book, I intend to help you navigate the experience of living intensely by helping you to examine the following questions:

▶ Is there something wrong with me?

▶ How does this trait explain my life experiences so far?

▶ What can I do now to heal some of the emotional wounds, improve my life and fulfil my potential?

▶ How do I go beyond 'surviving', and actually thrive as an emotionally sensitive and intense person?

Once you have discovered the origin of your differences, you can begin the journey towards retrieving your long-lost gifts. Suddenly, your life history will make sense. As you move towards self-actualization, themes such as authentic existence, meaning of life and purpose of being will come to the fore. When you step into your authentic truth, you will come to trust your unique way of relating to the world, and you will discover what you have to offer. Ultimately, I hope that you can come to see that, as a unique individual, your abilities and awareness are not only unusual, but also extremely precious.

## Intensity and personal growth

Perhaps no one has told you that, as an emotionally gifted person, it is natural for you to go through cycles of intense inner conflict, which sometimes look like 'emotional crises'. These cycles are neither random nor futile, nor are they a sign of emotional weakness. Instead, they are part of the critical process known as 'positive disintegration'. This concept comes from Polish psychologist Kazimierz Dąbrowski, who dedicated his life to studying the psychological structure of intellectually and artistically gifted people. His work confirms that emotional intensity is essential for the higher development of such individuals. The feeling of being torn in two is the split between your ideal self and your current predicament; it is intense because your growth requires you to tear down existing structures, including your way of thinking, feeling and being in the world.

Growth is to see what you have not seen, feel what you have not felt, do what you have not done. It requires you to relinquish who you thought you were, question the conventional life trajectory, and be plunged into a space of not knowing. You may also have to endure a period of loneliness, where you become out-of-sync with your peers, whose norms are incompatible with your new-found authenticity and higher values.

For emotionally gifted individuals, inner conflicts are developmental, rather than detrimental - they are 'growing pains'. According to Dąbrowski, after a period of 'positive maladjustment', you will be able to live in line with your higher values, such as forgiveness, authenticity and creativity (Dąbrowski, 1966). In other words, your emotional intensity is not just a byproduct of your growth, but an essential ingredient for it. Because of your intense nature and desire to be your best self, you are constantly on a steep learning curve, shedding the old to make space for the new. Even if you sometimes resent the challenges, your need for authenticity and fulfilment propels you forward.

At the core of each emotionally intense person, is someone who is immensely resourceful, passionate and has a lot to give. Your emotional intensity will not go away - but why would you want it to? Instead, you can learn to embrace it, and you can reject the conventional, medicalizing – and ultimately incorrect - view of your experience and adopt one which helps you to fulfil your potential.

# What makes this book different?

In recent years, interest in emotional sensitivity, empathy, introversion and other related subjects has surged in the field of psychology and in mainstream media. However, many questions remain. This book aims to fill a gap by offering an alternative perspective on the current perception of sensitivity in modern society.

### 'IT IS NOT JUST ABOUT AVOIDING BRIGHT LIGHTS AND LOUD NOISES': GOING BEYOND AVOIDANCE

As we review existing resources for sensitive individuals, we will most likely come across themes such as 'survival', 'protection' and 'avoidance'. Unfortunately, this approach paints a picture in which sensitive individuals are somehow 'too fragile for the world'. The advice focuses on managing overwhelm, such as to 'stay away' from stimulations, to set boundaries and limit contacts, and to avoid emotional vampires, etc. While there is value in such advice, it runs the risk of perpetuating the idea that sensitive people are inadequate in some way, or that they are not equipped for the world.

Emotionally sensitive people see and feel things deeply, and are highly attuned to what's happening around them, but this is only one aspect of their nature. They are not only sensitive, but also deeply passionate and loving. Many are extroverts who draw strength from being with other people. The key to a fulfilling life, therefore, does not lie in complete solitude and avoidance, or in a world devoid of all contact and stimulation.

Many emotionally sensitive and intense people are also gifted, and gifted people need some level of stimulation to maintain their optimal level of functioning. They feel most energized and connected when they are engaged in relationships with those who match their levels – intellectually, psychologically and emotionally. For them, both in life and in relationships, under-stimulation is just as problematic as over-stimulation.

If we identify ourselves as being somehow broken and incapable, and needing shelter and protection, we will have to design our lives in a way that is geared towards avoidance rather than growth and expansion. Eventually, our world shrinks, and we lose sight of our limitless potential.

In contrast, it would be much more helpful if we could focus on strengthening our resilience, to enable us to stay open and to go with the ebb and flow of life. What is proposed in this book is a different approach, which may seem counter-intuitive at first: rather than trying to find ways to defend ourselves against the inevitable challenges in life, we take the stance of openness. Instead of shrinking, we expand. Thriving as a sensitive person is about opening to the world, rather than closing down.

Our ultimate, collective goal should be to liberate the gifts within each of us so that we can all show up in the world and make our mark. This cannot be achieved if we are locked in a limited, fear-based way of being. Hence, I would like to invite you to completely turn around how you think of emotional intensity: you are not a helpless victim of your traits, and the world is not a 'me-versus-them' battlefield. Rather than reinforcing the need to shrink and hide, together we shall find a way to manifest as the passionate, loving and giving souls that we are.

## 'IT IS MUCH MORE THAN JUST EATING WELL AND MEDITATING': ADDRESSING PROBLEMS AT THEIR EMOTIONAL ROOTS

Currently, there is an abundance of resources offering lifestyle adjustment advice for sensitive people, such as ways to improve sleep and reduce stress through meditation, diet and nutritional supplements. Despite its practical value, this book aims to go beyond 'common sense' advice and explore in more depth the developmental trajectory and psychological impact of being sensitive, intense and gifted.

While it is not a disease, being sensitive comes with its challenges. In this book, we will address issues such as the pain of being misunderstood, the challenges of feeling different and out of sync, and how to deal with a spectrum of emotions from fear to shame. Although there will be some practical advice, this is not a problem-solving 'manual'. The most profound and lasting shifts come from a transformation of our mindset and our fundamental beliefs about ourselves and the world. We will confront the core memories that generate the presenting problems so that we can dispel emotional difficulties at their roots. What lies ahead of you is more than just an intellectual process: it involves changes on an emotional level. By combining traditional psychological theories with spiritual wisdom, the goal of our work is to help you uncover buried emotional pain points and to mobilize your innate capacity.

## WE WILL TALK ABOUT GIFTEDNESS

Being highly sensitive and intense is a common experience for most gifted people; as you will see in later chapters, most gifted people have above-average reactions to intellectual, sensual, physical and emotional stimuli, known by psychologists as 'excitabilities'. (Research shows that excitability is a feature of high developmental potential that often accompanies special abilities and talents.). However, very few have addressed the relationship between emotional intensity, sensitivity and giftedness, perhaps because 'giftedness' is such a loaded term in our society.

Giftedness is often misunderstood as narrowly defined by IQ. In fact, giftedness comes in all shapes and sizes and is much more than just intellectual capacities. Alongside exceptional abilities in the areas of music, visual art or sports, there are also the much less discussed interpersonal intelligence, intra-personal intelligence and spiritual intelligence.

'Gifted' is simply a word given to those who have a different neurological makeup and different needs in the world. Just like eye colour or height, it is a neutral, innate trait. Being 'gifted' does not mean you are superior, it may just mean that you are wired differently. Being gifted has its unique challenges, and we desperately need a safe space that is free from judgement and criticism, where we can talk about the many joys and sorrows that come with it.

# Let's begin

Reclaiming your identity as an emotionally and empathically gifted person means respecting your unique needs and, most importantly, not shaming yourself for being different. It is precisely your sensitivity and intensity that underpin your potential excellence. Thus, for the sake of your growth and those around you, it is essential that you embrace your true identity to reframe your unique qualities as assets rather than liabilities.

In this book, we will go through a series of reflective topics. Using a range of exercises, I hope to help you to arrive at new ways of thinking about your past, navigating your current life and creating new possibilities. The unique circumstances of your personal background, values and beliefs will show you your own path. Some ideas and concepts will resonate more than others, so please feel free to take only those you need, and leave the rest behind.

Imi Lo

www.eggshelltherapy.com

## Reflection prompts

Before you start, you may wish to reflect on the following questions:

1   Where are you at in your journey from healing to thriving?

2   Which aspects of your life call for the most attention right now?

3   What do you most hope to achieve by reading this book?

4   What kind of support might you need during this process?

5   What is the first step you would wish to take towards your
    psycho-spiritual growth?

# Part 1

## The emotionally intense person

In this first part of the book, we will explore the idea of emotional sensitivity and intensity. Perhaps, as an emotionally sensitive person, you have been dismissed as being 'over-sensitive' or 'too intense'. Perhaps, at times, you have even felt that there is something wrong with you; that your sensitivity is the symptom of an illness. In Chapter 1 we will look at some definitions – what exactly do we mean when we talk about 'emotional sensitivity' or 'emotional intensity' – as well as at some of the characteristics associated with being emotionally sensitive. We examine these ideas in more detail in Chapter 2, exploring such concepts as the highly sensitive person, giftedness, empathy, thin boundaries and introversion. Chapter 3 focuses on emotional giftedness: the different forms it takes and the traits exhibited by those who are gifted, and discusses the idea of over-excitability. Chapter 4 rounds off Part 1 with an exploration of the relationship between emotional intensity and mental health.

# Emotional sensitivity, intensity and giftedness

# Definitions

Throughout this book the phrases 'emotional sensitivity', 'emotional intensity' and 'emotional giftedness' are used interchangeably. This trait is defined by the following five core features:

1 Emotional depth, intensity and complexity

2 Deep empathy and sensitivity

3 Highly acute perceptivity

4 A rich inner world imbued with sensual, imaginary and intellectual excitability

5 Creative potential and existential angst

## EMOTIONAL DEPTH, INTENSITY AND COMPLEXITY

As a highly sensitive person, you have the capacity to experience emotions to unusual levels of depth, complexity and intensity. This makes you feel extremely alive, sometimes painfully so. You experience a constant stream of both positive and negative feelings, sometimes together, sometimes going from one to the other in a short period.

You experience powerful and fluctuating emotions: you may soar high into bliss and plunge low into gloom in rapid succession. When art or music moves you, you are flooded by waves of joy, or transcend into a state of ecstasy. Sometimes, emotions are so powerful and compelling that you feel out of control.

You are extremely passionate, even if you do not show it on the outside. Since you also feel love and attachment intensely, you tend to form a strong emotional connection with people, places and things, which sometimes makes separation and endings difficult.

You may experience life with more tenderness, melancholy and nostalgia than others. However, your emotional expansiveness is often misunderstood as a condition or emotional immaturity, rather than as evidence of your profound capacity to feel.

## DEEP EMPATHY AND SENSITIVITY

You have always had a grave concern for those around you, even from an early age. When others are abused or mistreated, you feel as if it is happening to you. Not only do you empathize with other people, but you may also feel a direct link to animals, nature and elements in the spiritual realm.

You have an innate ability to feel into other people's energy, and you identify with the traits of an 'empath'. In social situations, you intuitively know what physical or emotional state others are in; sometimes, you feel that you 'absorb' their physical and psychological ailments.

Because of your responsiveness and insights into others' pain, you tend to form soulful and meaningful connections. When it comes to relationships, you are loyal, idealistic and romantic. However, being naturally open and sensitive also means you are vulnerable to relational injuries. Your loving and compassionate nature may have been curbed due to early rejection and trauma.

Having a heightened sensory system also means that you are extremely sensitive to your surroundings. You have an increased appreciation of sensual pleasures, such as music, language and art, as well as intense reactions to sight, sound, touch, taste and smell. This can cause you to feel overwhelmed or uncomfortable with too much sensory input. You may be sensitive to loud noises, strong smells, or tactile sensations such as clothing tags and rough surfaces. You may suffer from physical symptoms such as misophonia (low tolerance of certain sounds), hyperacusis (sensitivity to certain frequency and volume ranges of sound), multiple allergies and pain sensitivity.

## HIGHLY ACUTE PERCEPTIVITY

Being perceptively gifted means you can sense and perceive things that others miss. With an acute awareness, you see beyond superficiality, and your mind is often busy grasping patterns and making connections.

Insights, intuition and the ability to read several layers of reality allow you to assess people and situations rapidly. You may be shockingly perceptive and accurate in noting the dynamics in social situations. You have a sense of knowing when something is about to happen, or about other people's inner worlds. You can sense when something doesn't add up, and the intentions, thoughts and feelings that lie beneath people's facades.

However, your abilities do not necessarily make life easy. Even though your insights and intuitions overwhelm you sometimes, you cannot 'un-see' things. You are bothered by hypocrisies and unfairness and struggle with inauthentic people and situations. You cannot help but be the one who points out the 'elephant in the room'.

Your perceptiveness comes with its challenges. Others may not welcome your insights, and you may seem intimidating to those who feel 'seen through'. Combining your introspective nature and your awareness of the suffering, hypocrisies and complexities of life, you may constantly feel older than others around you, like an 'old soul' that has somehow lost its roots.

In a family situation, you may be scapegoated to be the one who carries the painful truth that is unsaid while the facade of normality is maintained. Perhaps you have been assigned the role of being the 'problematic one', the scapegoat or the black sheep. Often, this is an unconscious strategy used by some family members to evade their own emotional pain and suffering.

You have an innate urge to push the boundaries of conformity, to question or to challenge traditions, particularly those that seem meaningless or unfair. Paired with a strong sense of justice, you are frustrated with corruption and inequality in the world. Being one step ahead of time, you reveal truths and progressive thoughts most people find unsettling to hear or see. Although this may mean a challenging life path for you, you also have the potential to thrive as a visionary leader.

### A RICH INNER WORLD, IMBUED WITH SENSUAL, IMAGINARY AND INTELLECTUAL EXCITABILITY
You have a rich inner world fuelled by imagination and inner dialogue, and saturated with words, images, metaphors, visualizations, vivid fantasies and dreams. As a child, you may have retreated to your imaginary haven in times of emotional turmoil.

Intellectually, you are inquisitive and reflective. You have a strong need to seek to understand, to expand your horizons, to gain knowledge and to analyse your thoughts. With an ability to process information with speed and depth, you absorb it very quickly. You may be an avid reader and a keen observer. You may appear critical and impatient with others who cannot keep up with you. You also have the ability to integrate intellectual concepts with your deep feelings for original ideas. You may have a constant stream of ideas, sometimes so many that you feel you cannot keep up with them.

You tend to experience zealous enthusiasm about certain topics and endeavours. When you get excited about an idea, you find your mind running faster than your words, or you find yourself talking rapidly, perhaps even interrupting others. When you become absorbed in your love for a piece of art, literature, theatre or music, the outside world ceases to exist.

You are highly capable of contemplative thinking and self-reflection. The flip side is that you may be occupied with obsessive thoughts, and scrupulous self-examination. You may suffer from perfectionism or being too critical of yourself.

Your openness to experience also means you have greater potential for spiritual insights and experiences. You are sensitive to the spiritual world, and perhaps were drawn to the spiritual path from a young age. This may or may not manifest as some form of psychic ability.

## CREATIVE POTENTIAL AND EXISTENTIAL ANGST
You have always been concerned with the big questions of life. From a young age, you may have experienced existential depression and felt grief over the meaninglessness of life, death and loneliness. You might have a difficult time fitting in with those around you, or feel frustrated that they are not prepared to consider these weighty concerns.

Your existential angst manifests as an unnamed sense of urgency, a constant impulse to move forward. You get a constant 'niggling' feeling that time is running out, or that there is something important that you should be doing, even when your vision is not clear yet. Perhaps you feel a weight of responsibility on your shoulders – even for things you are not responsible for. Such pressure can cause you to be highly self-critical, and experience anxiety, guilt and a sense of failure.

Your angst propels you to learn, to expand, and to advance along your life path, but it can also paralyse you. You may be prone to creative blockages such as 'artist's block', 'writer's block', procrastination, the fear of exposure or 'Imposter Syndrome' (the feeling that you are a fraud). Perhaps when you have a strong vision or innovative idea, you feel the split between belongingness and authentic expression – you want to express with your full, authentic self but you are worried that this means being rejected, or leaving people behind.

You may be a polymath, or a 'multipotentialite' – someone with multiple interests and creative pursuits, and not just one calling. You yearn to be of service to the world, but struggle to focus on one channel. Nevertheless, you have always known deep down that you are dissatisfied with a life that is meaningless and task-driven.

## The caveat

In this book, we embrace the concept of 'neurodiversity': that particular groups of the population are innately different from the norm, with a specific kind of sensitivity, intensity and giftedness. But my intention is NOT to create a grossly simplified system that forces your reality into a fixed pigeon hole, or rigidly suggests that you will always perceive, think or feel in a certain way.

The conceptualization of the emotional intensity trait inevitably involves some generalization and reduction of human complexity. Unfortunately, this is a limitation of language: just as a map is always a simplification of the territory it is trying to chart, to make sense of things and to communicate we need to create a schematized version of an intangible reality.

Though the typology is necessarily a simplification compared with a real, unique human being, a caricature is the last thing I want to reinforce. We must not forget that what always holds more weight than the theory is the 'here-and-now-ness' of a living human being, who is constantly changing and evolving. I hope we can all retain the wisdom of the 'beginner's mind', in that part of us will always stay open and curious, and see things as if for the first time.

Nothing is definite.

# What do we know about emotional sensitivity and intensity?

In recent years, there has been an increased interest among psychologists and the general public in emotional sensitivity, empathy, emotional intelligence, introversion, and the correlation between these traits and one's wellbeing and creativity. You might have identified yourself as a highly sensitive person, an 'empath' or an introvert. You might have wondered if your trait was a sign of mental illness or a result of childhood trauma. To start making sense of your life experience of being a sensitive and intense person, let's begin by reviewing some of these concepts, and how they may or may not relate to you.

## The highly sensitive person

Dr Elaine Aron's book *The Highly Sensitive Person* (1996) brought the concept of high sensitivity to prominence. According to Aron, 15–20 per cent of the population are born with 'sensory processing sensitivity' – a distinct trait with an incidence too high to be a disorder and too low to be mainstream.

Aron's research found that the highly sensitive person (HSP) has more activity in the right hemisphere of their brain, along with a more reactive immune system and nervous system. Those with high emotional sensitivities often experience physical sensitivities. What may be considered slightly aggravating to most people – things like crowds or the ticking of a clock – can be too much for HSPs, who react to high levels of stimulation, sudden change, and the emotional distress of others. To HSPs, loud noises, bright lights, humming televisions, and even the touch of clothing tags against the skin can seem overwhelming.

These sensitivities are identifiable from an early age. In most cases, highly sensitive children are labelled as weird, sensitive or shy. Their temperaments vary widely, depending on the way in which they are parented: the highly sensitive child may be labelled as difficult, active, unruly and demanding – or, at the other end of the spectrum, as almost 'too easy to raise' (e.g. too undemanding or adult-like).

These highly sensitive children – who are equally likely to be males as females – are often seen as perfectionists, since anything being 'out of alignment' may bring psychic or physical stress. This tendency towards perfection can show up as obsessive-compulsive tendencies. Up to 70 per cent of HSPs are introverted and require private time to rejuvenate and ready themselves to re-enter the hustle and bustle of modern society.

As a pioneer of the topic, Aron has played a major role in bringing awareness of emotional sensitivity to the mainstream media. In the 20 years that have passed since the publication of *The Highly Sensitive Person*, countless books and articles have been written about HSPs, and the specific issues they face, such as romantic relationships and finding peace and success in the workplace. These resources may provide relief for the sensitive individual who is finally able to put a name to their experience. However, many questions remain unanswered: how can one alleviate the deep-rooted psychological wounds that come with growing up different? How does sensitivity relate to other personality attributes, such as empathy or intelligence?

## BEYOND THE HSP

You may be thinking 'The characteristics of an HSP seem to describe me to a tee. How does this book differ from others on HSPs?'

I have expanded the definition of emotional sensitivity to include a dimension of intensity and giftedness. In my research and clinical work, I have found that there is a group of people – perhaps a subgroup of HSPs – who are not only 'sensitive', but also exceptionally intense, passionate, perceptive and creative. If you are one of these people, the term 'sensitivity' is simply inadequate to describe your experiences.

In the dictionary, a sensitive person is 'capable of perceiving with a sense or senses, responsive to external conditions or stimulation, susceptible to slight differences or changes in the environment'. Those who are sensitive are 'easily irritated, predisposed to inflammation' and 'easily hurt, upset, or offended' (*American Heritage® Dictionary of the English Language*, 2011). Although this traditional definition of sensitivity captures your ability to be highly aware of your surroundings, it only showcases the reactive and passive aspects of your personality.

In contrast, here is the dictionary definition of intensity: 'having great energy, strength, concentration, vehemence, etc., as of activity, thought, or feeling', and having 'a high degree of emotional excitement; depth of feeling' (www.dictionary.com). Being emotionally intense means you are not only sensitive, but also full of passion, emotional energy and vigour.

You may possess a rich and complex inner life and relish fine or delicate tastes, scents, sounds and works of art. Because of that, you are acutely aware of the subtleties of your environment. HSPs are usually highly empathic and can sense what needs to be done in a given situation to make others comfortable. Your sponge-like ability to soak up information makes you sensitive to the moods of others. However, you are not only sensitive but also passionate – perhaps an idealist or a romantic. In your most natural state, you feel vividly alive. On a regular basis, you have a taste of ecstasy.

Another issue that is worth considering, beyond the current advice for HSPs, is energy and stimulation management for the emotionally intense and sensitive. In the original HSP definition, sensitive individuals are described as those who are easily startled or rattled, and they are advised to rearrange their lives to avoid upsetting or overwhelming situations. It is believed that change can shake up the HSP, and competition or observation can lead to nervousness or shakiness (except for a small sub-group of 'sensation-seeking' HSPs who thrive on novelty and risk). As a result, most HSP self-help books focus on managing over-stimulation, and many therapists and coaches who work with HSPs concentrate on offering guidance on how to limit external stimuli and stressors (Aron, 2013).

However, emotionally intense and gifted people are not necessarily stimulant-phobic. In fact, they need a certain degree of stimulation to maintain their optimal level of functioning. To be physically and psychologically well they must also be generative and creative, and to have found their 'sweet spot' of balance where they can consistently enter a creative 'flow' state (see Chapter 10). Yes, they need to be mindful of the level of stimulation they let into their life, but they must also avoid being under-aroused. Under-stimulation is just as problematic as over-stimulation and can have ramifications in all aspects of life, including work, loving relationships, and daily activities. This book will tackle the issues that arise at both ends of the spectrum. For instance, we will explore how life partners who 'under-stimulate' the gifted brain can present unique challenges. The key to the health and wellness of the emotionally intense person is to find the right intellectual, emotional and physical stimuli, rather than merely trying to avoid them.

## Giftedness

Very few existing works on sensitive people acknowledge their emotional power as a gift. In fact, Dr Aron herself was reluctant to associate the concept of high sensitivity with giftedness: she considered sensitivity to be a neutral trait, but regarded giftedness as a 'highly positive' one (Aron, 2004). However, I must disagree with Dr Aron in her view of 'giftedness' as a necessarily superior or 'highly positive' trait. Like 'sensitivity', it merely describes a characteristic which differentiates a part of the population from the norm. The definition of 'giftedness' as an ability to express talent in a way which the world recognizes as outstanding is a narrow and limiting one. Giftedness does not necessarily equate with skills or any externally distinguished achievement, it is a trait that comes with strengths and perils, just like sensitivity. Dr Aron observes that not all HSPs are gifted and that not all gifted people are HSPs. Though this is true, increasing clinical and anecdotal evidence is proving that there is a huge overlap between these two groups.

Many intense and sensitive individuals demonstrate characteristics that researchers see in the gifted population. Gifted people are powerful processors, absorbing and digesting sensory and emotive information at high speed. In turn, their levels of perceptivity – and the accuracy of their intuition – are beyond the norm. As with the gifted, keen powers of observation and extraordinary perception are often found in emotionally sensitive and intense individuals.

Moral sensitivity is another trait the gifted possess. For the morally sensitive, many emotional triggers concern issues that are bigger or deeper than their immediate surroundings. For instance, what on the surface seems to be a run-of-the-mill upset related to a work situation, may make the morally sensitive person uneasy with injustice (discrimination, sexism, etc.) or with the perceived gap between the way things are and how they ought to be. In young people, moral sensitivity may show up as a rebellion against seemingly trivial matters or as a strong passion for humanitarian or revolutionary ideals – concerns which the adults around them are unable to comprehend.

The emotional struggle the gifted go through is called 'positive disintegration' (Dąbrowski, 1966). They are not 'suffering' from their sensitivities, but are using them instead as a tool to expedite their growth – whether or not they realize what they are experiencing. When the gifted person experiences personal growth, they go through a period of difficulty as their pre-existing, dysfunctional worldview and self-limiting beliefs are shattered. In the end, they can emerge as more rounded human beings, capable of independent thought and ways of living.

Rather than only teaching you how to manage emotional overspill or over-arousal, I would like to propose a fundamental shift in the way you view yourself. I hope you will come to see that most of your intense emotional processes are not at all pathological, but are all serving a purpose and driving towards growth.

In later chapters we will also see that the reluctance to explore the relationship between emotional sensitivity, intensity and giftedness has an adverse impact on not just the intense person but the progression of our collective consciousness as a whole.

## Empaths and empathy

Self-help and esoteric literature uses the term 'empath' to describe people who are sensitive to the emotions and energy of other people, animals and the environment. Although there is not one unified definition of an empath, they are usually described as individuals who have the ability to physically feel the energy field of others and their surroundings. Their empathic skills can sometimes appear 'psychic' or mystical.

Although the term 'empath' has not been used very much within academia, psychologists have studied extensively the concept of empathy. In psychology, empathy is broadly defined as the ability to share or understand another person's feelings, and it determines how we conduct ourselves in this world (Davis, 1983). When studying what it means to have high empathy, psychologists have found the following:

► Individual differences in empathy levels affect the way people recognize facial expressions (Besel and Yuille, 2010) and react to social cues (Eisenberg and Miller, 1987).

► Individuals with high empathy are better at identifying emotions in others. However, they also have a 'bias' towards negative emotional expressions, meaning that they are more sensitive and alert to negative feelings in others. Perhaps because of this, those with high levels of empathy are also more likely to experience 'empathic distress' (Chikovani *et al.*, 2015).

► Interestingly, women with high empathy are better than their male counterparts at noticing and recognizing sadness.

► Excessive empathy – an intense sharing of others' negative emotions – is linked to emotional disorders in health professionals and caregivers. Their empathic distress is often framed as compassion fatigue or burnout (Batson, 1987; Eisenberg *et al.*, 1989; Gleichgerrcht and Decety 2013).

As an empath, you possess a natural gift for making instant connections with the emotions of others – and this all happens automatically and unconsciously. If you fail to realize this – and to distinguish your feelings from those of others – you can become overwhelmed with undue stress and pain from those around you. Mental symptoms like mood swings and physical symptoms such as unpredictable energy levels, headaches and fatigue can result. Therefore, it is critical that naturally empathic people learn to hone their empathic skills such as emotional regulation and perspective taking (McLaren, 2013). Without these skills, many empaths end up 'absorbing' the emotions of others to the point of burnout (see Chapter 12).

## Having thin boundaries

In the 1980s, Dr Ernest Hartmann (1989, 1991) developed his 'Boundaries in the Mind' concept that explains individual differences in sensitivity levels. In his theory, he proposed a spectrum of personality types with varying boundaries – thick to thin.

Dr Hartmann began his research with the observation that people who have frequent nightmares shared certain personality traits. These nightmare-prone individuals tended to be more 'undefended,' artistic, imaginative, and open to experience. The barrier between their self-identity and the outside world was relatively permeable, and therefore he characterized this group of individuals as having 'thin boundaries.' At the other end of the spectrum, those with thick boundaries were described as being more 'solid', 'stoic' and 'persevering'.

Since Dr Hartmann's discovery in the 1980s, at least 5,000 people have taken his Boundary Questionnaire (BQ) and more than 100 published papers have referenced it. Research is mounting to build a picture of the issues and symptoms that are associated with the 'thickness' of one's mind boundaries.

People with thin boundaries are highly sensitive, and may demonstrate the following from an early age:

▶ Reacting more strongly to sensory stimuli and becoming agitated by bright lights, loud sounds, and particular aromas, tastes or textures.

▶ Responding more strongly to physical and emotional pain in themselves and others.

▶ Becoming stressed or fatigued due to an overload of sensory or emotional input.

▶ Having a higher likelihood of suffering from allergies or having highly reactive immune systems.

► Experiencing deeper reactions to childhood events.

In contrast, people with thick boundaries are often described as stoic or thick-skinned, and may tend to:

► Brush aside upsetting emotions so as to solve any problems at hand or to get practical matters in order.

► Have less-apparent mood swings.

► Be slower to recognize how and what they are feeling.

► Be less sensitive towards subtle changes or nuances in their environment.

► Experience an ongoing sense of detachment or (sometimes) emptiness.

A unique aspect of this concept is its relationship with physical health. It has been found that thick-boundary people are more prone to hypertension, chronic fatigue syndrome and ulcers, whereas thin-boundary people are more susceptible to migraines, irritable bowel syndrome and allergies. There also appears to be a relationship between thin boundaries and multiple chemical sensitivities (Jawer, 2006).

Another interesting research correlation is found between boundary thickness and people's career choices. Art students, music students, male and female fashion models, and mixed groups of creativity-oriented employees tend to have significantly thinner boundaries (Hartmann, 1991; Krippner, Wickramasekera, Wickramasekera and Winstead, 1998). It has been suggested that people with thin boundaries are more likely to have been involved in and to have benefited from psychotherapy (Hartmann, 1997). In their work 'Your emotional type', Jawer and Micozzi (2011) even invented a framework that allows readers to access treatments which are most likely to be effective by looking at where they lie on the mind-boundary spectrum.

Despite its limitations – namely, a lack of quantitative data and inevitable generalizations – the idea of mind-boundaries offers a useful framework that can help differentiate and explain the variance in individual personalities. The difficulties experienced by a person with thin boundaries are not dissimilar to those experienced by the emotionally sensitive or hyper-empathic. Without awareness and scientific research, it is easy to imagine how thin-boundaried, sensitive people might have been plagued by misunderstanding and confusion for many years.

## Trauma-induced environmental sensitivities

In their seminal work *Healing Developmental Trauma*, Heller and LaPierre (2012) discuss the idea of 'energetic boundaries' and how environmental sensitivities can result when these boundaries are compromised.

Our energetic boundaries constitute the three-dimensional space that is above us, below us and around us. It buffers us and regulates our interaction with other people and the environment. We are all to some degree aware of the impact of a compromised physical body – try imagining someone standing too close to you on public transport. However, unlike physical boundaries, energetic boundaries are invisible. Thus, the experience of a boundary rupture can be puzzling and distressing. For instance, you may not be able to recognize clearly when and how your energetic boundaries are being violated.

People with an intact sense of boundaries are able to feel safe in their own company, and have a capacity to set appropriate limits with others and the world around them. However, if you experienced a chronic early threat, you may struggle to fully develop your sense of these energetic boundaries. As a result, you may become extremely sensitive to your surroundings. Sometimes, you can appear to be psychic and are able to energetically attune to others and the environment. Other times, you can feel swamped or invaded by other people's energies and emotions. Damaged boundaries can also lead to the feeling of 'spilling out' into the environment, not knowing the difference between self and other, or inner and outer experiences.

Environmental sensitivity is a telling sign of having compromised energetic boundaries. Because intact energetic boundaries are needed to filter environmental stimuli, without them you may feel extremely raw, as if you are 'walking around with no skin'. You will feel constantly flooded by environmental stimuli, including 'human contact, sounds, light, touch, toxins, allergens, smells, and even electromagnetic activity' (Heller and LaPierre, 2012, p. 157). In their 'checklist' Heller and Lapierre also include physical symptoms such as multiple allergies, migraines, chronic fatigue syndrome, irritable bowel syndrome or fibromyalgia as signs of having compromised boundaries.

The inability to filter external stimuli makes the world seem continually threatening, leading to a constant state of tension and hyper-vigilance. As a result, you may feel the need to isolate yourself. As you don't have an adequate internal sense of safety and energetic boundaries to count on, you may have resorted to isolating yourself, or limiting contact with others in order to feel safe.

In Heller and LaPierre's theory, these environmental sensitivities are a result of an impaired capacity for connection to oneself and others, due to early developmental trauma. They also suggested that these sensitivities are related to complications at birth, prenatal trauma such as intra-uterine surgeries, prematurity with incubation, or traumatic events during gestation. The downside of this perspective towards sensitivity is that it can be pathologizing.

However, as demonstrated by the research on HSPs, sensitivity is not a disease. It is an innate trait, a temperament that one is born with. Although some research and theories have linked sensitivity with childhood trauma, the relationship between the two remains unclear. The topic of childhood trauma in relation to the emotionally sensitive child will be addressed in Chapters 5 and 8. For now, it is important that we do not assume a direct link between childhood trauma and sensitivity in an overly simplistic and linear way.

# Introversion

It is important not to confuse emotional sensitivity with introversion.

The main difference between introverts and extroverts is the source of their energy. Extroverts get energy from their environment and the people around them, while introverts tend to revive in solitude or inner reflection. Introversion has recently been popularized by Susan Cain's book *Quiet* (2013) and her TED talk (www.ted.com/speakers/susan_cain). Like the emotionally sensitive, introverts as a population have long been sidelined. In *Quiet*, which has been translated into over 30 languages and made bestseller lists in several countries, Cain explains how the brain chemistry of introverts and extroverts differs, and how society ultimately misunderstands and undervalues its introverts. Her book helps introverts to understand themselves and take full advantage of their strengths.

The highly introspective nature of the emotionally gifted means that many of them are perceived as introverts. As keen observers of the world, they learn about life through their evaluative thinking and ability to quickly absorb sensory information. Like well-developed introverts, they are less likely to be rash and jump into things and can find the wisdom and strength to deal with the challenges of the world through introspection and self-evaluation.

Research on introversion repeatedly finds that introverts are more sensitive than extroverts (Koelega, 1992). In fact, it has been suggested that the description of 'introversion' is almost identical to what has become the standard definition of high sensitivity – deep thinkers, preferring to process slowly, sensitive to stimuli, emotionally reactive, needing time alone, and so forth. But it is important to note that not all HSPs are introverts. According to Dr Aron, roughly 30 per cent are social extroverts.

This chapter has given you an overview of the existing prominent theories about emotional sensitivity, intensity and giftedness, and how they relate to one another. These knowledge frameworks are invaluable for the insight they provide into who you are and your life history. By reviewing past events and difficulties with newfound self-knowledge, you can adopt a new perspective and realize where some of the hurtful, uninvited commentary others have made about you might have come from. Regardless of the traits that you identify with, your goal should always be to own who you are authentically and to find a way of living that meets your needs and honours your strengths.

# 3

# Emotional intensity and giftedness

Gifted people are global and sophisticated thinkers, who have a unique psychological structure. They possess a greater capacity and thirst for knowledge and discovery, experience enhanced sensual stimuli, and feel a full range of emotions to an immensely deep level.

As discussed in Chapter 2, giftedness has become a loaded term in our society, and that makes owning it difficult. Perhaps you have always been aware of your unique ability in certain areas. You may have the capacity for strong, accurate 'gut' instincts about people and events, or maybe you can astutely observe others to gather extensive sensory information from your surroundings – but you have never considered these abilities 'gifts'.

We live in a world that glorifies rational 'head' intelligence. This intelligence is more valued than 'personal' intelligence or the more intangible, heart-based wisdom, such as heightened capacities for empathy, justice, moral sensitivity, reflectiveness, self-knowledge and a drive towards personal growth.

In this chapter, we will explore the link between emotional intensity and giftedness, and how your sensitivity and perceptivity are gifts in their own right.

## The giftedness that no one talks about

Exploration of giftedness dates back to the 19th century. It stems from the study of individual differences in intelligence within the fields of psychology and philosophy. Before 1972, there was one – and only one – criterion to identify giftedness: the IQ test. However, researchers soon found this metric to be limiting: IQ tests assess analytical and verbal ability, but fail to measure a broad range of skills that are critical to life, including practical knowledge and creativity.

During the 1980s, psychologists began to devise new models of giftedness. Françoys Gagné is a pioneer in the field. In his theory, 'The Differentiated Model of Giftedness and Talent', he differentiates between giftedness and talent, proposing that giftedness represents innate abilities, while talent is something that is systematically developed with education, guidance and training. In his work, gifts, or natural abilities, fall into the following five categories: intellectual, creative, socio-affective, sensorimotor and 'others' (e.g. extrasensory perception) (Gagné, 1985, pp.103–12).

At around the same time, Harvard researcher Howard Gardner (1983) noted the importance of 'personal intelligence', such as interpersonal skills and the ability to reflect. He used the concept of 'Multiple Intelligences' (MI) to raise awareness of additional potential strengths outside of the existing conventional ones. These forms of intelligence include linguistic, logico-mathematical, musical, spatial, kinaesthetic, interpersonal (people-smart), intra-personal (self-smart), naturalistic and existential.

As the study of individual variations and our understanding of human capacity has evolved, the term 'gifted' no longer solely refers to intellectual capacity. Gradually, teachers and parents are accepting the idea that advanced abilities can occur within any subject or discipline, such as maths, science, language arts, sports and more.

Despite the expansion beyond IQ, however, current conceptions of giftedness rarely mention emotional giftedness. Many emotionally gifted individuals do not fully see or celebrate their introspective gifts because they are not lauded by society. Although their abilities may be expressed as deep thinking, profound empathy, or self-reflection, there is no official metric to measure them. Most educators focus only on outwardly visible and quantifiable markers: emphasis is placed on the rank, the performance and the portfolio, and the 'gifted' child in school is the one who gets high grades or wins competitions and awards.

Children are taught to be 'head smart', but no one explicitly teaches them how to develop their 'heart wisdom', and there are no textbooks, trained tutors or coaches to harness these gifts. As a result, young people endowed with emotional gifts are not supported and are often left struggling on their own. They can sense that they are somehow different from the others, but no teachers or parents have told them why or how to manage their abilities. Inevitably, many begin to believe that there is something wrong with them. Sadly, our existing model that mainly uses outward performance to identify the gifted is hugely limiting and detrimental to the evolution of our collective human intelligence.

To expand our perspective, let's look at some forms of emotional giftedness and why it is a critical part of human potential.

# Forms of emotional giftedness

### EMPATHIC AND PERCEPTIVE GIFTEDNESS

In his 'Multiple Intelligences' model, Gardner characterizes 'interpersonal intelligence' as the ability to understand various qualities of others. From an early age, children with high interpersonal intelligence show instances of empathy, unselfishness and consideration for those around them.

These highly empathic and perceptive children feel and appear more mature than their peers because of their sensitivity, responsiveness and insight into others' pain. They may feel overly responsible, guilty and helpless if they fail to alleviate the distress experienced by those around them. This quality may result in them falling into the role of the confidante, the counsellor, or even the saviour within the family.

Because of their heightened perceptivity, they may be the only one who sees through the guise of normality and propriety in their surroundings. They are lonely, frustrated or disappointed because the adults around them are engaging in a facade; or, they feel guilty about having these perceptions.

The capacity for deep empathy and insight into others' inner states also brings about a level of moral sensitivity that is beyond their years. These children show superior ability to think about global ideas like justice and fairness. Being so intensely aware of world issues and the feelings of others can make them vulnerable to being overwhelmed. In addition, they have to face adult reactions that do not meet their expectations. For example, they may want to help the poor and homeless by giving away their possessions but cannot comprehend their parents' reluctance to do so.

## INTROSPECTIVE GIFTEDNESS

Apart from a high sense of empathy and perceptivity, Gardner proposes another kind of 'personal intelligence' known as intra-personal intelligence. This is defined as the capacity to be introspective. This intelligence is essential for attaining a developed sense of self and a high level of inner wisdom. Introspective individuals are keenly and accurately aware of themselves, and they have a higher-than-normal degree of self-knowledge. Gardner (1983, p. 252) describes the intra-personally gifted as someone who engages in constant and continued development where they strive to become increasingly autonomous, integrated or self-actualized. The end goal of these developmental processes is a self that is 'highly developed and fully differentiated from others'.

Gardner's description of these individuals parallels Dąbrowski's 'Theory of Positive Disintegration' (1966). In both theories, being introspective and self-critical are not disorders, but essential vehicles for growth. It is in their intensified manner of experiencing, examining and analysing themselves that the gifted grow faster than the average person. These individuals consistently experience, in their whole being, the painful split between who they want to be and who they are now; the experience of this gap is what prompts them to take positive action towards psycho-spiritual growth. These inner forces also often generate overstimulation, conflict and psychic pain that are misinterpreted as illness. It is precisely this ability to go through sometimes painful self-examination that enables their multi-dimensional development towards higher levels. In other words, their intense emotions are not disorders but the impetus for growth. It is their willingness and courage to engage in such processes consistently that makes them uniquely gifted.

## EXISTENTIAL GIFTEDNESS

In addition to the eight forms of intelligence in his model, Gardner wrote about a ninth intelligence: the existential

(Gardner, 1995). Existential intelligence is defined as 'a concern with ultimate life issues'. The core ability of this intelligence is the capacity to associate oneself with the existential features of the human condition, such as the significance of life, the meaning of death, the ultimate fate of the physical and psychological worlds, love of another person, or total immersion in a work of art (Gardner, 1999).

Someone who possesses a high level of existential intelligence is always asking the big questions such as: 'Who are we?', 'What is ethical and what is not?', 'Where is humanity heading?' or 'Is there meaning in life?'. Their giftedness may express itself explicitly in leadership or spiritual roles (preachers, theologians, ministers or yogis), as well as secular roles (philosophers, writers, artists, scientists, or others who address broad, complex questions as a part of their profession).

As children, the existentially gifted may have a difficult time fitting in with those around them who are unable to comprehend their concerns and may dismiss them. Their teachers and parents may fail to answer their questions about profound aspects of life.

The existentially gifted are more likely to experience a high degree of existential angst. Being aware of the finite quality of life and their potential, they constantly feel compelled to move forwards. This can manifest as strong creative urges, but also as constant restlessness, anxiety and insecurity.

The existentially gifted are idealists as they consider the limitless possibilities of how things could be. They are on a constant quest to connect with something larger than themselves and seek answers about the obligations, opportunities and mysteries of human life. It pains them to see how the world is falling short. They may challenge existing values and traditions as well as any inconsistencies and absurdities they see in the world around them.

Unfortunately, especially when they are young, if the existentially gifted person tries to share these concerns with others, they are met with responses that range from apathy to dismissal to hostility. They soon realize that most people are more concerned with the mundane; thus they feel internally isolated and end up keeping their thoughts and feelings private until they find a community that shares their humanitarian concerns, or a space that celebrates their particular interests and values.

## SPIRITUAL GIFTEDNESS

This dimension is often missed because for a long time we have lived in a society that values what is concrete and measurable. Although we are all capable of and can work towards spiritual awakening, the spiritually gifted often show, from their early years, a particular kind of openness and sensitivity towards the transpersonal realm. Spirituality can have nothing to do with organized religion, but rather it represents a direct connection we have with everything in this world and a sense of transcendence.

Researchers Edward Robinson (1983) and Edward Hoffman (1992) have extensively studied spiritually gifted individuals. Intensive examination of hundreds led them to conclude that spiritual giftedness is not something that one outgrows. Indeed, there is such a thing as an innate aptitude for having spiritual experiences. People who have this aptitude are able to see the bigger picture, and perceive things on a symbolic level that is beyond the concrete and literal. They are also able to feel a connection between themselves and the universe. (Piechowski, 2001).

A communion with the spiritual dimension can manifest itself in various ways. It may be distinct changes felt in the body, infusion with a sense of strength that is beyond oneself, a strong sense of 'pulsating energy with all living things' (Piechowski, 2006, p.257), or the feeling of being in harmony with the universe. Spiritual experiences among the spiritually gifted fall within these themes: unity, oneness, ecstasy, timelessness, and the interconnection of everything (Piechoski, 2006; Lovecky, 1998).

Children with spiritual gifts often have the ability to induce heightened consciousness through meditation or fantasy play, show wisdom that seems beyond their years, and feel strongly connected to the world around them, their inner self, other people and God (however 'God' is defined) (Piechowski, 2006). Sadly, more often than not, spiritual aptitude creates more difficulty than ecstasy for the spiritually gifted child. Usually, when the child tells an adult about intense spiritual thoughts, the adult tells the child it's wrong to have such 'ideas'. The stricken child is then led to devaluing their experiences, instincts and perceptions. In the worst cases, they begin to believe that they are 'crazy' and internalize an enormous amount of shame that they carry into adulthood.

Many individuals may not necessarily recognize their spiritual inclination for what it is. Nonetheless, they are drawn to transcendental experiences and are more likely to make room in their lives for them rather than to drown in the mundane. They may encounter many moments of awe or deep appreciation of beauty in the arts of nature, show an ability to use spiritual wisdom to solve problems, and naturally engage in virtuous behaviours with gratitude, forgiveness and compassion.
Even if they do not name it as such, it is precisely their ability to enter these states more readily than others that make them spiritually gifted.


# Personality traits of the gifted

After decades of research and debate, scholars have now come to agree with the notion that giftedness is best defined as a kind of 'asynchronous development', where one's inner experiences and awareness are different from the norm. The domain of asynchronous development can go from creativity to intellectual capability, and certainly includes special abilities in perceptivity and sensitivity. Annemarie Roeper, an expert in the field, helped bring together many of the various theories with her concept that 'giftedness is a greater awareness, greater sensitivity, and a greater ability to understand and transform perceptions into intellectual and emotional experiences' (Roeper, 1982).

According to Mensa (America Mensa Ltd., 2017), gifted individuals possess the following qualities:

- ▶ Unique perception and awareness
- ▶ A sense of humour and creativity outside the norm
- ▶ Intuitiveness
- ▶ Insightfulness
- ▶ Relentless curiosity
- ▶ Heightened creative drive
- ▶ High sensitivity, an acute awareness of complexities and consequences and the expectations of others
- ▶ Easily excited
- ▶ Possible consistent high energy level
- ▶ A regularly activated nervous system.

Many gifted individuals have abilities in many areas, known as 'multipotentiality'. They can often move fluidly from one pursuit to another, though this is often misunderstood by others as being noncommittal.

They are idealists: they strive for moral integrity and take an interest in social reforms.

They are perfectionists: they may be highly self-critical, struggle to tolerate mistakes, and have trouble taking credit for their achievements and contributions.

They have a high need for a sense of freedom and autonomy. Although they yearn to be a part of the group, they also need to live in line with their values. This means many of them experience the conflict between authenticity and maintaining traditional relationships.

Last but not least, the gifted have an intense moral commitment to bettering the world. They want to address the injustice they see and are frustrated with inequality in humanity.

In essence, giftedness is a lot more about *who you are*, rather than *what you do*. It is not measured by the outward marker of success or achievement. Indeed, sometimes, the traits associated with giftedness may prevent a person from achieving outward success. For example, an emotionally sensitive and gifted child may not be able to focus on their schoolwork due to being more deeply affected by a conflict with peers, or concerns about their parents' looming divorce. They may also be more interested in their reading, seeking answers for humanitarian affairs, or helping others. These children will not demonstrate their giftedness in a conventional way, but that does not make them any less gifted.

As adults, the gifted also face unique challenges as others do not necessarily understand their specific needs. Dr Mary-Elaine Jacobsen (2000) has identified some of the main criticisms faced by gifted individuals:

▶ 'Why don't you slow down?'

▶ 'You worry about everything!'

▶ 'You are so sensitive and dramatic.'

▶ 'You are too driven.'

▶ 'Who do you think you are?'

# Over-excitability

To understand giftedness, we cannot omit discussion of the concept of over-excitability (OE). The term 'over-excitability' is derived from a Polish word which literally means 'superstimulatability' (Daniels and Piechowski, 2009). It represents an expanded awareness and a heightened capacity to respond to stimuli of various types. OE is innate and observable from infancy. Emotional intensity and sensitivity are often a direct manifestation of emotional OE, but gifted individuals often experience emotional OE with other types of OE.

### EMOTIONAL OE
This is the OE that is the most closely associated with our topic. Emotional OE is reflected by extremes of complex emotions, high empathy and strong identification with others' feelings,

and powerful and passionate emotional expression. In children, emotional OE is often the first to be noticed by parents. These children may seem exceptionally insightful and perceptive, often beyond their years. When unmanaged, it can also emerge as mental illness, such as existential depression and panic attacks. Other manifestations include physical responses like stomach aches and blushing, or psychological signs such as a concern with death, and depression.

Emotionally over-excitable people have a remarkable capacity for deep relationships; they show strong emotional attachments to people, places and things (Piechowski, 1997). Those with strong emotional OE are acutely aware of their feelings, of how they are growing and changing, and often carry on inner dialogues and practise self-judgement. People high in emotional OE are sometimes accused of 'overreacting', and their intensity is often misunderstood as a sign of emotional immaturity. Their compassion and concern for others, their focus on relationships, and the intensity of their feelings may also interfere with everyday tasks and hold them back from achieving in life (Piechowski and Colangelo, 1984).

It has become increasingly clear to most researchers that intellect itself cannot ensure one's higher development or self-actualization: emotional intensity 'of significant strength' (Silverman, 1993) must also be present.

## INTELLECTUAL OE
The gifted are more driven by the search for understanding and truth than by academic achievement. They seek solutions and find it difficult to let go of a problem. Sometimes their excitability is evidenced by a love of intense discussion and debate, multiple intellectual interests, and complaints of being easily bored (Clark and Zimmerman, 1992; Freed, 1990; Lovecky, 1998; Piechowski, 2006).

## PSYCHOMOTOR OE
Psychomotor OE is a heightened excitability of the neuromuscular system. It may include a love of movement for its own sake, surplus of energy demonstrated by rapid speech,

enthusiasm, and a greater capacity to be active and energetic. (Falk *et al.*, 1999).

## SENSUAL OE

Sensual OE is often overlooked in the study of the gifted. Sensual OE refers to a heightened responsiveness to sensual stimulus. People with high sensual OE are drawn to sensual pleasure, aesthetic appreciation and a desire for physical admiration. Gifted people with sensual OE may develop a love for particular textures of clothing or food, take immense delight in particular smells, have strong memories of and associations with food or have an intense reaction to beauty. On the flip side, strong sensual OE can show up in an intense aversion to noises or smells, or in allergies (Silverman, 1993).

## IMAGINATIONAL OE

Imaginational OE is expressed through the capacity for vivid imagery in the mind, dreams, fantasies and creative inventions. People with high imaginational OE have extraordinary visualization abilities: they may dream in colour, be exceptionally inventive, and have a love for poetry, drama, music and art. Sometimes it is difficult for them to express their thoughts in words because they think with images and metaphors. Gifted children often have imaginary friends (Piechowski, 2006; Roeper, 2007), and many hide in their imaginary worlds as a way of coping with difficulties in reality.

# Reclaiming your giftedness

After reviewing the above theories and descriptions, I hope you have reconsidered what it means to be gifted.

Do you identify with some of these gifts or traits? While analysing your life's course, did you demonstrate some characteristics of giftedness, especially in the domain of interpersonal/intra-personal intelligence?

'Giftedness' refers to much more than IQ and intellectual capacities. Being 'gifted' does not mean you are superior, it may just mean that you are wired differently. It is important that you recognize your giftedness in order to live authentically, and that you don't beat yourself up when you find that you express yourself differently or possess specific needs that the majority of others don't share or understand.

You may feel unable to reclaim your identity as a gifted person because of the social stereotype that the gifted are somehow above everyone. That is not the case; owning your giftedness is not about arrogance, but rather the need to be congruent with your capabilities, values, and place in this world.

# Emotional intensity and mental health

# What is normal?

Society has a particular standard of what 'normal' is. Traditionally, researchers have either paid little attention to the idiosyncrasies of those who do not fit nicely into the norm or, worse still, regarded them as pathological. Even in the field of psychology, only Dąbrowski's theory of emotional development has acknowledged the gifts within those who experience emotions intensely. However, with the advancements made in technology and medicine, more and more scholars and scientists have come to acknowledge the idea of 'neuro-diversity' as a reality. The concept of neuro-diversity recognizes that there exists infinite variation in the way our minds and brains are wired as a species and that the idea of a 'normal' or 'healthy' way of being in this world is simply a cultural construct.

Intense people have abilities and possess traits that differ from that which is 'neuro-typical'. In that sense, they live outside the dominant societal standard of what is 'normal'. As an intense person you might experience life differently to those around you, and there are many ways in which you might be misunderstood. For example, you may find it difficult to comply with certain social conventions or standard procedures – especially if you fail to see the meaning in them – and others may render your stance as rebellious or non-compliant. In a conventional institution, your inquisitiveness and curiosity may not be welcomed. The variety of diverse interests you have might be regarded as showing a lack of focus, or as being disorganized. Your innate ability to gather information and perceive a variety of possibilities can make it hard to be patient with the way things are, and your ability to think critically about yourself and others may make you seem intolerant. For all these traits, you are labelled 'too much', or deemed 'excessive'. However, what is construed as neurotic or extreme for someone else may be natural for you. As we have seen in the previous chapter, it is a well-established fact that gifted individuals possess increased levels of emotional, imaginational, intellectual, sensual and psychomotor excitability. Perhaps it is not that you are too 'sensitive', or too 'much', it is the world that needs to come up to speed with the power and experience of those blessed with psychological velocity and complexity.

Since most people, including those in the mental health profession, lack accurate information and awareness about sensitivity and intensity, the most creative, forward- and independent-thinking people are being mislabelled and misdiagnosed. Your strong feelings are misunderstood as bipolar disorder, and the extreme and intense mood swings – combined with frequent complications in relationships and strong emotional reactions – can look like borderline personality disorder. It is important we understand that not everyone who experiences emotions intensely has a mental disorder – it is only the rigidity and lack of flexibility that constitutes an illness. Furthermore, in psychiatry, a 'diagnosis' merely represents a cluster of symptoms which are the manifestations of internal conflict and disease. The real distinction from one disorder to another is, in truth, unclear. These arbitrary categories exist so that clinicians can fall back on a standardized framework in which to conduct research or to prescribe medication. In some parts of the world, they serve a purpose for the insurance industry. This dominant medical model is a limited framework and can lead us to overlook the possibility that psychological distress may simply be the result of us not honouring our utterly unique make-up as individuals.

To further examine the relationship between mental distress and emotional intensity, we will take a closer look at one of the most common diagnoses (or misdiagnoses) that is given to emotionally intense individuals: emotionally unstable personality disorder (EUPD), more commonly known as borderline personality disorder (BPD).

# Borderline personality disorder and empathy

Despite being referred to as a 'personality disorder', BPD reflects not a character flaw but a limitation in a person's capacity to regulate emotions. It usually begins during adolescence or early adulthood and involves extreme emotional reactions in the context of unstable relationships. The person with BPD may also experience frequent mood swings, or a chronic sense of internal hollowness, and they may use impulsive self-soothing behaviours to manage these symptoms. Research into understanding BPD is still ongoing, but the consensus is that both genetic and environmental influences constitute its cause.

It is increasingly being recognized that many people who receive the diagnosis of BPD are endowed with heightened sensitivity and perceptivity. What was previously thought of as a genetic vulnerability may, in fact, be a form of exceptional ability. Research has found that individuals with BPD seem to possess an uncanny sensitivity to other people's subconscious mental content – thoughts, feelings, and even physical sensations. They also appear to have a talent for influencing others (Park *et al.*, 1992). It was found that individuals with BPD showed a heightened sensitivity to non-verbal cues when compared with people without BPD (Domes, Schulze and Herpertz, 2009). A well-known study, for instance, looked at the way in which people with BPD react to photographs of people's eyes compared to those without BPD. The researchers found that the BPD group was more able to guess correctly what emotions these eyes expressed, showing their enhanced sensitivity to the mental states of others (New *et al.*, 2012).

Although the link between BPD and empathy remains controversial, many people with BPD identify with the traits of an 'empath', or of being hyper-empathic. An empath is extremely sensitive to the emotions and energy of other people, animals and places (Orloff, 2017). Psychologists have found that individuals with high levels of empathy are more reactive to social cues (Eisenberg and Miller, 1987), better at recognizing emotions in others, and are more likely to experience 'empathic distress': compassion fatigue and burnout (Chikovani *et al.*, 2015). Despite their enhanced empathic ability, however, people with BPD have difficulties navigating social and interpersonal situations. Without the capacity to regulate their emotions and manage attachment in relationships, their hypersensitivity turns up as emotional storms and mood swings (Fonagy, Luyten and Strathearn, 2011). Though they possess such a gift for reading others, those with BPD may be easily triggered by stressful situations and suffer a constant fear of abandonment and rejection (Fertuck *et al.*, 2009). This phenomenon is known as the 'borderline empathy paradox' (Franzen *et al.*, 2011).

# The relationship between sensitivity and mental illness

The relationship between an emotional gift and mental illness is a complicated one. In some cases, high empathy is an outcome of growing up in a traumatic and unpredictable childhood environment. Many people with BPD have a history of abuse, neglect, or prolonged separation from their primary caregivers in childhood. Some studies show that a high percentage of individuals with the disorder reported being abused (Zanarini, 1997). In response to maltreatment and neglect, these children learned to 'ramp up' their empathic functioning to protect themselves. They were trained by their environment to become highly attuned to the subconscious cues given out by the adults they depended on so that they could prepare for any unpredictable behaviours.

Environmental factors alone, however, cannot fully explain the occurrence of a mental disorder. Sometimes, siblings who grow up in the same household are not always affected identically. Thus, we must also consider the biological and innate temperament-based factors that influence one's distinctive reactions to traumatic events. As psychologists Bockian and Vilagran (2011, p.30) suggested, 'It is extremely unlikely that someone with a placid, passive, unengaged, aloof temperament would ever develop borderline personality disorder.' Child psychologists have found that there is a subset of children with a heightened sensitivity to the social world, whose developmental and emotional outcomes are critically dependent upon their early childhood conditions (Tschann *et al.*, 1996). Where there is early trauma, it is this group of children who are at risk of developing mental illnesses.

In other words, severe difficulty in emotional regulation is not a direct result of being born intense, but a result of two combining factors:

1 Being born with heightened sensitivity and a gift in perceptivity.

2 Living in a deficient childhood environment that fails to meet emotional needs.

Under favourable, 'good enough' circumstances, a child who is born sensitive and intense would not grow up to have severe emotional difficulties. However, if their primary caregivers lack the capacity to attune themselves with their child, or even resent or feel threatened by their unusually perceptive child, their abuse and neglect can sabotage the child's healthy development. Attachment theories tell us that children will do all they can to preserve a good image of their parents because, at a young age, it is impossible to think of the people we depend on as 'bad' (Winnicott, 1960). Thus, even when their parents are incompetent, abusive or neglectful, children naturally blame themselves.

Some research found that ongoing negative feedback towards the young person's intuitive perception is the most damaging (Park et al., 1992). If the parents explicitly or implicitly reject the child's idiosyncrasies, the child will internalize the shame of rejection and experience themselves as being profoundly bad (toxic shame), and their natural gifts in perceptivity become hijacked by negative bias and projections. Without an environment where they can learn to set healthy boundaries and experience secure attachments, they are deprived of the opportunity to learn how to self-soothe and regulate emotions. Even as adults, they continue to live with a fear of abandonment, betrayal and rejection, and a profound sense of internal hollowness.

Sometimes, even with the best intentions, emotionally intense people and their parents do not realize or acknowledge that they are gifted, and are therefore not aware of the impact of their over-excitabilities. When the child goes through life feeling out-of-place without knowing why, they can quickly draw the conclusion that something is wrong with them – leading into a vicious, depressive cycle that escalates into an actual clinical disorder.

We are not here to dismiss the validity of all mental health diagnoses, or the importance of appropriate treatment in the case of severe psychological trauma. But it is important to examine the root of your suffering: often, it may be a reflection of your natural tendencies, and a result of being misunderstood, rather than as a sign of defectiveness. We must be extra cautious to not reinforce any restrictive categories, diagnoses and stigma around emotional intensity.

Even if you do struggle with managing your emotions or toxic shame, I hope that you can reconsider your life narrative: your struggles are not your fault, and the shame that you carry is a natural reaction to a childhood environment that has not sufficiently supported you. With the right knowledge and skills, you can learn to ride the waves of life's ups-and-downs with both passion and peace. Your psyche always wants to move in the direction of healing and integration. Even if you have been wounded, once you can begin to recognize and trust your fundamental goodness, restoration and integration will naturally start.

Though history cannot be changed, you can rewrite the story that you tell yourself. You are in no way 'bad' or 'too much'. You are a sensitive, intuitive, gifted individual who might have been deprived of the right kind of nourishment during childhood. Your high level of awareness and acuity to subtleties is both rare and incredibly precious. If you listen to the voice of reason and truth within – the voice that, though at times faint, always knew that you were not fundamentally wrong – you can work towards liberating yourself and retrieving the long-forgotten gifts inside you.

# Part 2

## The complexities of being emotionally intense

In Part 2, we will explore some of the common issues that arise with being emotionally intense. The pain that comes from a pervasive sense of being 'too much' is not to be taken lightly. Many emotionally intense adults have lived their lives believing that there is something wrong with them, and feeling lonely and misunderstood. With an extraordinary emotional depth from a young age, they have grown up feeling and being different from others. As an emotionally intense person, your perceptive abilities and empathic gifts may have made it difficult for your early caregivers – even those with the best of intentions – to care for you and nurture your unique qualities. In Chapter 5, we look at what can happen when parents who, due to their own vulnerabilities or limited intellectual or emotional capacity, are not able to provide an adequately supported childhood. Being part of a minority, and faced with the pressures to be like the rest of society, you may feel the internal conflicts and even guilt for being different. Perhaps for your whole life, you have been caught between two contradictory desires: the desire for acceptance, and the desire for authentic expression. In Chapter 6, we look at this perennial struggle of 'truth versus tribe'. We will explore what it means to be different, and the challenges of trying to be fully you – sensitive, intense and passionate, while finding a safe sense of belonging in the world. In Chapter 7, we will look at some of the emotional difficulties you as an emotionally intense person may face, such as toxic shame attacks, feeling out of control, and sometimes, paradoxically, feeling numb.

# At home

# The invisible wounds

All children have certain undeniable physical and psychological needs. They have the right to safety, to be protected from harm, to receive love and attention, to be spontaneous and playful, to have their needs heard and recognized, and to have appropriate supervision, boundaries, and guidance. On top of these fundamentals, emotionally gifted children face unique challenges, for example with sensory sensitivity and emotional regulation, such that they require a deeper level of understanding.

The developmental differences for sensitive children usually become apparent before 18 months old. From as young as a pre-verbal age, they can sense that the way they experience the world is fundamentally different from their family. They may feel an omnipresent sense of feeling like a Martian visiting the Earth, and this feeling of lacking a 'shared reality' with those they depend on – for example, their parents – can be terribly unsettling and frightening. Also, due to their natural perceptivity, they are more acutely aware of and have more intense responses to what happens to them and around them, which may exacerbate the impact of any childhood difficulties.

Parenting a sensitive and gifted child can be incredibly rewarding, but it requires a high level of maturity and awareness. Unfortunately, not all parents are equipped with these skills. In fact, many parents of sensitive children are not intentionally abusive or exploitative, but their struggles or limitations have kept them from sufficiently fulfilling their roles. For some sensitive children, their gifts are not celebrated but seen as threats or symptoms of a disorder. For many others, their parents simply do not have the capacity to comprehend their exceptional nature or to adapt to their unique needs.

Childhood wounding does not always take a physical form. Our society typically recognizes the horror of physical child neglect, but not the emotional pain that comes from inadequate or deficient parenting. Psychological damage can happen in all sorts of subtle and invisible ways, from a caregiver's lack of awareness, subtle put-downs, neglect, and allowing toxic sibling rivalries, to over-control and restriction of the child's freedom and independence. From the outside, these parents may manage to fulfil all the requirements society sets regarding primary care, such as providing clothing and schooling, yet in these cases, the lack of outside corroboration of what is happening can make the invisible wounds more psychologically damaging. In some homes, there is even the pressure to maintain the illusion of a happy family to 'save face' or protect the family name. If your parents and society told you that you were loved, yet you did not feel it, this discrepancy could create immense confusion or a sense of guilt for not feeling as loved as you should be.

The problem is further complicated if your parents were themselves vulnerable. Perhaps they did not set out to be abusive or neglectful but were held back by trauma and difficulties in their own lives. As a sensitive child, likely profoundly gifted with heightened sensitivity, compassion and maturity beyond your years, you may have felt protective of your parents. When you saw their vulnerabilities, your default position would have been to defend and protect them. However, this protective instinct has held you back from acknowledging the truth of what was lacking in your childhood. You may be reluctant to speak about the issue for fear of attacking your vulnerable parents or caregivers. Perhaps when any question is brought up, you jump to their defence and claim that they simply did their best and meant no harm.

Of course, not all sensitive and gifted children were inadequately parented, and our aim here is not to criticize or blame parents. It is likely that they tried their best using the knowledge, resources and capacities they had. At the same time, however, the effect of having inadequate parental support can neither be pushed aside nor does it simply disappear, as a myriad of psychological consequences will inevitably erupt in later years. This chapter might be a difficult read, but it will help us to understand the impact of not having our emotional needs met. It is critical that we do not fall into the trap of simplistic or linear thinking, of blaming or victimizing. Instead, let's see this as an opportunity to come closer to ourselves and our inner truth, and to make room for new insights that will help us heal and grow.

# Forms of invisible wounds for the emotionally sensitive child

'Just because they didn't mean it doesn't mean it didn't hurt.'

To be emotionally and developmentally injured, the wounds you carry did not come from a single traumatic event, but from a pattern of traumatic events or a dysfunctional family dynamic. Here are some of the psychologically damaging family patterns commonly faced by an emotionally sensitive, intense or gifted child.

### ROLE REVERSAL

According to Heinz Kohut (2009), the psychologist who specialized in understanding the development of our 'sense of self', certain needs must be met for a child to grow and develop. One such step in a child's development is to 'idealize' their parents. At least for a period, children must believe that their parents are powerful, knowledgeable and emotionally robust people who they can depend on. At an early age, it is by looking up to and admiring the adults around you as figures of power that you get to internalize a sense of strength and learn to find your way in this ever-changing, complex world. If, however, your caregivers were absent, vulnerable, or otherwise erratic, then you would have been deprived of such an opportunity.

Psychological studies have found that when faced with life's challenges, people who have internalized a powerful parental figure will be able to adequately sooth themselves, while those who lacked dependable parental figures are easily traumatized and experience negative emotions for longer periods of time (Kerns, 2007). Of course, no parent is omnipotent or omnipresent: absences and let-downs inevitably happen. The real difference between adequate parents and those who are not lies in whether they have enough stability to contain – to a degree – their personal stress. Did your parents possess a robust support network and the inner strength so as to not seek emotional support from you? Did they demonstrate at least some degree of resilience and the ability to bounce back from life's challenges? Or did they consistently allow an emotional overspill where you felt you must step in as a rescuer?

In her seminal work *The Drama of Being a Child*, psychologist Alice Miller (1995) describes how parentification is sometimes a result of parents using their child to fulfil the needs that were not met in their own childhood. These parents inappropriately depend on their empathically gifted children to provide them with mental and emotional support as well as refuge in unconditional love. Doing so places the child in an impossible position of having to be responsible for their parents' happiness and well-being.

When parents lack the stability to lead their family, it is often their emotionally gifted child who steps up to take over the caring role. This role reversal in the parent–child relationship is known as 'parentification'. Parentification can be when the child is made responsible for physical and concrete tasks such as grocery shopping or taking care of younger siblings, but more often, it means meeting other family members' emotional needs, such as serving as a companion, mediating conflicts, and providing support and comfort. In some situations, your intuitive gifts and natural interpersonal intelligence might have been the only thing that kept your family together. The burden of these responsibilities – that should rightfully belong to the adults – forced you to grow up too fast, too soon. In a way, you were both your own parent and also your parents' parent, giving you no one to look up to, seek guidance from, or learn from. Defenceless, and unsupervised, the world might seem like a terrifying place.

As a result of parentification, you have learned to reduce and repress your needs to make room for others at home, to the detriment of your freedom and growth. While your energy was devoted to playing counsellor for others, you might have missed out on the times where you should be allowed to be playful, spontaneous, make mistakes, and focus on nothing more than your own growth and learning.

## SCAPEGOATING

If your family life from childhood leading up to today were being put on stage, would there be a kind of 'fixed role' assigned to you? For example, are you 'the responsible one', 'the golden girl', or perhaps 'the emotional one', 'the strange one' or 'the black sheep'?

Theorists of Systemic Family Therapy use the term 'Identified Patient' (Minuchin *et al.*, 1975) to describe the scapegoated person within a family with an unhealthy relationship dynamic. Of the many types of childhood injury, being scapegoated is one of the most insidious. Often, pointing the finger at one person as the cause of all evil, is an unconscious strategy used by some family members to evade their own emotional pain and suffering.

The scapegoat role is not assigned by accident. It is often imposed on the innately sensitive and hyper-empathic child because they often are the 'whistleblower' who sees through and points out the facade. As the family members 'discharge' their resentment, the child becomes the carrier of all the angst and suppressed negativity in the family.

Once the pattern is set, the family typically goes to great lengths to keep the dynamic that way – the scapegoat must remain the scapegoat – otherwise, the others would be forced to face their own vulnerabilities. What this means is that when the scapegoat tries to walk away from this toxic dynamic, they may be met with subtle or not-so-subtle emotional revenge, manipulation or blackmail.

Here are some of the signs that you have been scapegoated in the family:

▶ Your parents treat you differently from your siblings.

▶ Your mistakes are blown out of proportion or punished disproportionately.

- ▶ Your parents do not intervene or take notice when you are being bullied by others.

- ▶ You always have the feeling that you 'don't fit in' with your family, and you didn't develop strong connections with them.

- ▶ When you thrive, get stronger and more independent, you sense that your family members are intent on bringing you down or dismissing your achievements.

- ▶ You are bullied by your siblings, or they 'jokingly' mock you for your idiosyncracies.

- ▶ Name calling – you are always 'the weird one', the 'wild card', or 'the trouble'.

- ▶ Your family do not know who you truly are beyond the superficial, and have shown little interest in knowing.

- ▶ You are criticized for your natural attributes, such as your artistic or sensitive nature.

When this happens, it may not mean that your family members do not love you, or that they are intentionally trying to harm you. Rather, their need to label you often comes from their vulnerabilities and the fear of their own inadequacies.

Children naturally find their identity in what is reflected back to them by their parents. If your parents always treated you as the 'guilty one' or the 'responsible one', you might have found it hard to shake off this 'identity' in later life. Even when you eventually cut away from this destructive family dynamic, you may still carry with you mental or emotional repercussions caused by living out such a role. As an adult, you may have trouble feeling safe in relationships, due to the early betrayal of trust in your family. You may intellectually understand that you are not the cause of problems in your family, but to shift the internalized shame requires deeper emotional healing.

The healing journey back from being the scapegoat can be a challenging one, where you zig-zag your way from denial to anger, and eventually freedom and release. However, you must realize that the cause of chaos is not you, but your family's repressed anger and disappointment, and it should never have been your responsibility as a child to resolve anything. Once you can let go of this, and reacquaint yourself with people who see and cherish you for who you are, then you are on your way to living a vibrant and authentic life of your own.

## THE EMOTIONALLY STUNTED PARENTS

Research has found that an important factor in the emotional development of children to a great extent lies in how warm, responsive and emotionally present their caregivers are. Just being physically present is not enough: they must be attuned to the children's emotional states by providing feedback and connection.

In some cases, however, often due to their unresolved trauma, bereavement, and depression, the caregivers are emotionally stunted and cut-off. They are afraid of emotions and tender feelings and thus fail to connect with their emotionally intense child.

To fully understand the importance of emotional attunement, you may wish to watch a short video on YouTube of the 'Still Face Experiment'. In the experiment conducted in 1975 by Edward Tronick, a mother was asked to keep a blank face and not respond to her child's attempts to engage with her. When the baby received no emotional responses, he 'rapidly sobered and grew wary', made repeated attempts to interact with his mother, and – when his attempts failed – withdrew and turned away with a hopeless facial expression (Tronick, 1975). Though these events happened so fast that they were almost invisible, this study is a powerful indicator of the power of a parent's consistent emotive attention. Since the original study, the 'Still Face Experiment' has been thoroughly tested and replicated, demonstrating that the impact of parental unresponsiveness is profound and far-reaching. Babies are not born with the ability to manage their emotions. Instead, they need to learn such skills by having another person provide them with emotional feedback. Without it, they are left with a sense of chaos, shame, dread, powerlessness and despair.

Children do not need to be severely abused; merely having no one to see and hear them for who they are can leave them psychologically damaged. You might have been clothed, fed and educated, but your parents' robotic demeanour might have meant that you did not feel loved on an emotional level. If your parents were emotionally unavailable, they might have lacked the capacity to respect your intensity and natural passion. In fact, the depth of your feelings might have frightened them.

## THE UNSEEN CHILD

For children to develop a sense of self-worth – a sense that they matter in this world – they must first have their parents validate their fundamental worthiness. This need is known as 'mirroring': children need to be shown by their parents, both explicitly and implicitly, that they are special, wanted and welcome. Mirroring can be achieved by explicitly praising, applauding, acknowledging and valuing the child, but it is the more subtle clues – gestures, expression, tone of voice – that can most often demonstrate to a child that they are loved.

No parents can be the perfect mirror all the time – after all, there will be times when they are not able to be there for their child. This too is natural, and not a problem if misattunement does not happen often and if the child is not left alone for too long. Children who have been sufficiently well-mirrored can draw on their own memories and internalize the positive messages from their parents into a healthy and stable sense of self. With enough good mirroring experiences, the emotionally healthy child will no longer need others to reassure them how good they are. As adults, they will have a firm sense of self-esteem and a belief that they are fundamentally good. If, however, the parents' emotional distress or insecurities meant that the child did not get enough mirroring, the development of their sense of self would be disrupted.

A lack of mirroring and deep acceptance from parents is particularly detrimental to the development of sensitive and intense children, who need active support for the differences they already experience among their peers. Perhaps your parents only praised you for what aligned with their values, or when you performed well in your caregiving role – but not for who you are. If your parents only rewarded you when you conformed to their standards or fulfilled their needs, but did not support your growth towards your unique self, you might have come to the conclusion that your real self was not lovable, leading to deep feelings of worthlessness and insecurity in adulthood.

## Results of having an inadequately supported childhood

**DIFFICULTIES IN REGULATING EMOTIONS, STRESS AND IMPULSES**
Naturally, infants are not born capable of controlling their emotions, hunger or fear. To grow, young children seek warmth, comfort and closeness from their parents. When this emotional support is not available, their body's physiological system becomes activated and releases cortisol, the 'stress hormone'. When this becomes chronic, the child's brain development is negatively impacted. The parts of the brain that are responsible for 'executive function' – planning, emotional regulation and impulse control – become impaired.

As a naturally intense and excitable child, it was of particular importance to you that your parents modelled and taught you how to be aware of your physical needs, and how to manage stress and to regulate emotions. You needed your parents to allow you the room to learn, grow and explore the world while also teaching you how to find your limits with adequate discipline. Without this emotional feedback and practical guidance, you might have been left not knowing how to navigate life and may, therefore, find yourself struggling now with issues such as mood regulation, anger management, impulse control issues or eating disorders.

**LOW SELF-ESTEEM**
If as a child you were unable to internalize a deep sense of love and security, you might now carry a persistent feeling of being not good enough – that you are somehow disgusting, ugly, stupid or flawed. This may involve internal thoughts such as, 'Nothing I do is good enough', 'There is something fundamentally wrong with me', or even 'I am bad and toxic'. In more extreme cases, your low self-esteem can turn into self-hatred.

## EXCESSIVE SELF-CRITICISM

Sensitive children with inadequate support often grow up to be adults who are very hard on themselves. No one is perfect and we are all prone to mistakes, but since this message was not given to you as you grew up and warm forgiveness was not modelled and not internalized, you might have become hyper-vigilant about mistakes and failures in life.

## LONELINESS AND DESPAIR

If as a child you felt 'unseen' and not welcomed into the world, your ability to connect with both yourself and others may have been stifled. You may now feel a sense of profound isolation, and experience both an intense need for and an extreme fear of contact. If you begin to feel that no one can connect with the depth of your feelings or see you for who you are, you may end up with the feeling of despair.

## FEELING UNGROUNDED AND POWERLESS

The lack of a genuine connection with your significant others can derail your relationship with not only yourself but also the rest of the world. Physically, you may feel ungrounded and uncentred; psychologically, you may feel disconnected, unnourished and unsafe, as if you were a frightened child in an adult's body.

## MISTRUSTING THE WORLD AND HYPER-VIGILANCE

A child's early experiences have a powerful impact on how they see themselves and the world around them. If you have experienced the role reversal which placed you as the 'little adult' in your family, you had no one you could depend on. Being overburdened, you were conditioned to anticipate threats and stressors, which left your nervous system in a constant state of arousal. Unable to relax, you might have felt like you were always on the look out for danger, and this might mean that you now suffer from insomnia, irritability, jumpiness, and a host of anxiety-related disorders or obsessive-compulsive tendencies.

## INTERNAL HOLLOWNESS AND EMPTINESS

If your parents were neglectful or emotionally unavailable and failed to provide enough mirroring and attunement for your sense of self to fully develop, you may never be quite sure of who you are or where the boundaries are between you and others. Because you never really had the time and space to find out about your wants and needs and to grow into your authentic self, you may experience a sense of internal emptiness.

On the other hand, because the neglect you endured was so painful, you may have employed dissociation as a way of coping (you might also have learned this as a strategy from your dissociated parents). Dissociation may involve disconnection from the body, emotions, and other people. You can continue to function in the outside world, but with a lingering feeling of internal deadness and numbness.

### CHRONIC GUILT AND SELF-DENIAL

Children who are parentified often grow up struggling with a sense of guilt and the lingering fear that they are, and never can be, 'enough'. Their 'failure' in rescuing their parents – their inability to take away their distress – becomes toxic guilt. They may become overly centred on others, to the detriment of their own health and well-being.

They may become self-sacrificing: they listen to others but never take up space; they take pains to care for others while depriving themselves. They may have an overdeveloped sense of responsibility, which can put them at risk of being trapped in destructive relationships where they take on responsibility for others' maltreatment and bad behaviours.

## Journal exercise: family dynamics

Let's check in for a moment. Settle into a quiet place, and reread the above descriptions of various family dynamics in a receptive way. Notice your body's response to them. Does your deeper mind resonate with some more than others? Does your mind want to pull away from some of them?

Jot down notes in your journal, or in an exercise book, on your emotional and physical responses. Notice how reflecting on your childhood impacts your perception of yourself, your relationships and the world at large.

If developmental inadequacy or toxic dynamics were present in your childhood, the process of reviewing your past can be tough and can trigger strong feelings. Resisting this process is natural and understandable.

At the moment you look into your painful past you must also, paradoxically, cope with sadness, anger and grief over what has been missing. Although we are not able to go back and change the past, recent discoveries in the field of neuroscience can provide us with the hope that we may recover from the impact these early deficits might have had. The continuing plasticity of the brain means that nourishing, healthy relationships and positive experiences can help heal these relational wounds. Despite what may have happened in the past, you have a choice now. By allowing yourself to acknowledge the pain of deprivation courageously, you can begin to reclaim your space, your voice and your place in this world.

# In the world

# Standing out

Being different as an intense person can bring about difficulties that have nothing to do with the trait itself, but arise from being a minority group in society. To begin the journey towards understanding who you are, you must understand the degree to which your capacities have set you apart.

Most people are born into a world of quiet conformity, yet your natural idiosyncrasies do not allow you to hide. Being extra sensitive means you often see and hear what others do not. By default, you stand out from the crowd, sometimes painfully so. As a child who developed faster than others, being particularly insightful and perceptive may have made you more vulnerable.

Perceptively gifted children are often exceptionally aware of the suffering, hypocrisies and complexities of the relationship and social dynamics around them. They see and notice things that are beyond their years. They may be the only one in their family who knows what is going on beneath the surface appearance of normality and propriety. However, since they have not learned when and how to deliver these 'inconvenient truths' to people around them, they may point out things that the adults are not prepared to hear, and end up getting dismissed and shamed. Even as adults, gifted individuals struggle with hypocrisies they see in social situations. They may feel compelled to point out the truth, or feel unable to play 'the game'. Often, their high level of integrity becomes a threat to the group's status quo. Sadly, the result is that others might feel threatened and either consciously or unconsciously engage in behaviours that aim to squash the gifted souls.

Exceptionally conscious people are like canaries in a coalmine. In the old days, miners took canaries down the pit so that if poisonous gas was present, the canaries would show signs of distress, or even die. This warned miners of the danger. Like many creative artists, emotionally gifted people reveal truths and progressive thoughts most people find unsettling to hear or see. Humans tend to resist changes in the status quo; those who stir things up, who challenge the status quo, who make waves, are rejected by others who fear the unknown.

# Envy and the social dynamic around the gifted

One of the most insidious and destructive energies that impact the emotionally gifted – though it often goes unacknowledged – is envy. Unfortunately, our society does not always celebrate those who stand out. Embedded in the shadow of our collective unconscious is the belief that another person's success diminishes our own. While jealousy and envy are normal human emotions, they become destructive when they are acted upon.

Envy as an emotion is not in itself bad or negative. Benign envy is the feeling that we get when someone has the capacity and quality that we want in ourselves, and this type of 'emulator envy' can be productive as it points us to our values and propels action.

Toxic envy, however, is disturbing and damaging. Envy is also different from jealousy. According to psychoanalyst Melanie Klein, jealousy is more of a benign wish to have certain qualities or possessions, or the fear that what one possesses will be taken away (Klein, 1984). Toxic envy, however, is the desire to spoil what someone else has in the most negative manner. In other words, toxic envy is not just the angry feeling that another person possesses and enjoys something desirable, but also the impulse to destroy it for them.

The prevalence of toxic envy in groups mainly affects gifted and intense individuals; they tend to be the ones who draw attacks and ridicule, either explicitly or implicitly. In social situations, a group may work together to undermine the status of the gifted person to equalize the power dynamic. As James Fenimore Cooper said, 'The tendency of democracies is, in all things, to mediocrity (Cooper, 1838).

Outliers – people who stand out – inspire envy; such a phenomenon is real and pervasive, but we rarely talk about or acknowledge it, perhaps because somehow we feel that admitting that we can 'attract envy' is arrogant. The following concepts capture the social dynamic that commonly evolves around individuals who stand out (Tall Poppy Syndrome), the mentality that drives it (Crab-in-the-Bucket mentality), and how it manifests on a socio-cultural level (the Law of Jante). Becoming aware of these phenomena will help you to make sense of your experience and to recognize it when you have been on the receiving end of others' envy and projections.

## TALL POPPY SYNDROME

Tall Poppy Syndrome is a term used to describe the situation in which people who stand out in a group are resented, attacked and ridiculed. The name comes from Livy's *The History of Rome* (1884), which tells the story of a son, Sextus, putting to death all the important people in his town after his father symbolically cuts off the heads of all the tall poppies in his garden. This term is better known in the UK, Australia and New Zealand, but as a human behaviour in social groups, it is universal.

Tall Poppy Syndrome shows up in groups as young as school-age children. A study done in 2014 on young Australian high-performance athletes revealed that all female participants experienced bullying, from taunts, teasing, name-calling, alienation, judgemental comments, body language, gossiping, to ostracism (O'Neill, Calder and Allen, 2014). Unfortunately, many parents and teachers are not equipped or prepared to protect or to nurture a naturally gifted child. Many exceptionally perceptive children are even bullied by a less-than-gifted teacher. Parents can also be intimidated by their child's extraordinary ability and perceptivity, sometimes out of the worry that they will outshine their siblings.

## THE CRAB-IN-THE-BUCKET MENTALITY

The Crab-in-the-Bucket mentality refers to the animalistic behaviour of crabs in a competitive situation. Apparently, when more than one crab is in a bucket, none will escape. This is because when one crab finds its way to the top, the others will pull it back down. Unfortunately, such behaviour is typical in the human world.

Often done so subtly and out of an unconscious sense of shame or inadequacy, people have a tendency to diminish or negate the achievement of other individuals who stand out. This 'If I can't have it, neither can you' mentality comes from a primitive part of our human psyche. Underlying it is the poverty mindset – the belief that life is a big pie to be allocated. If there is only a limited amount of prestige, resources and attention to be shared in this world, then status becomes a relative concept – if there is a rise in one place, it will create a fall somewhere else.

## THE LAW OF JANTE

A commonly used phrase in Scandinavian cultures, the Law of Jante is a list of implicit rules that governs the way people think and act. As a concept, it was created by the author Aksel Sandemose in a novel called *A Fugitive Crosses His Tracks* (1933).

Within the Law of Jante, there are ten 'rules':

1 You're not to think you're anything special.

2 You're not to think you're as good as we are.

3 You're not to think you're smarter than we are.

4 You're not to convince yourself that you're better than we are.

5 You're not to think you know more than we do.

6 You're not to think you're more important than we are.

7 You're not to think you're good at anything.

8 You're not to laugh at us.

9 You're not to think anyone cares about you.

10 You're not to think you can teach us anything.

(Sandemose, 1933; English version in Trotter, 2015)

The Law of Jante gives an example of how the fear of the tall poppy can manifest itself on a wider level and penetrate all layers of our cultural rituals and behaviours. Those who transgress these unwritten 'rules' are faced with negativity and hostility. The embedded message these gifted individuals receive is, as Paulo Coelho (2006) puts it: 'You aren't worth a thing, nobody is interested in what you think, mediocrity and anonymity are your best bet. If you act this way, you will never have any big problems in life.' It is no surprise that these implicit Scandinavian norms has negatively affected the development of gifted adolescents in Sweden. A study measured how Swedish teachers felt about talented students and a variety of negative emotions appeared, such as that they are elitist and disrespectful of authority (Lindberg and Kaill, 2012).

Aggressive acts stemming from envy are deeply embedded in the bedrock of human behaviour, creating the most insidious and toxic dynamics that bring down those who stand out. Such acts are driven by fear-based thinking and worldviews. Back in the days when humans lived in small tribes, humiliating or sabotaging a prestigious member of the group could serve to balance out the group hierarchy, and therefore maintain a false sense of an egalitarian ideal. However, as the human species evolves, we ought to adapt to a new social system where a wide variety of individual differences is accommodated. In truth, people are infinitely different in their genetic make-up, strengths, desires, motivations and more. By stressing moderation and humility, and negatively portraying individuality and success, we discourage any progressive way of thinking and acting, to the detriment of creativity and the evolution of our collective consciousness. In the next section, we look at how these social dynamics impact on emotionally and empathically gifted individuals.

# Hiding and shrinking

## THE FROZEN GIFTS

After years of being criticized for being 'too much', and being on the receiving end of toxic envy, bullying and attacks, many emotionally sensitive and gifted people have learned to stifle or cover up their exceptionalities.

At some point in your life, to protect yourself, you had to 'hide and shrink'. However, what starts out as an attempt to self-preserve and stay safe, without awareness, can gradually be internalized as an inner reality. Rather than pretending that you are small, you come to BELIEVE that you do not deserve a place in the world. As you try to censor and silence yourself, you feel anxious about taking up any space in the world, or even secretly wish that you could disappear.

Many gifted individuals suffer from 'Imposter Syndrome' – an inability to internalize success. Instead of celebrating your achievements, you may have the feeling of being a failure, a fraud or an impostor. You may live in constant fear of being 'found out', and prefer to 'play safe', avoiding exposure to competitiveness and intellectual challenge, thus preventing yourself from achieving your full potential.

If you see being 'gifted' as an uncomfortable burden, you may develop a fear of success. You may not recognize your tendency to hide and shrink on a conscious level. However, on a subconscious level, the young child who feared ridicule, who needed to belong, who was traumatized by the bullies, may still be running the show and sabotaging your achievements in life.

When you try to squeeze your wild passion and spirit into a metaphorical prison, you will suffer from internal tension and pains. This may manifest not only as emotional distress but also as physical aches and pains. Some of the common symptoms are migraines, chronic fatigue, and debilitating allergies. Problems such as anorexia, obsessive–compulsive disorder and migraine headaches are often symptoms of a stifled gifted voice.

As you have disengaged with the part of you that is, in essence, passionate, excited and idealistic, you may end up feeling disconnected, empty and frustrated. You may also experience a spiritual crisis later in life, in which you feel that something important is missing, or feel plagued by a sense of meaninglessness.

The 2013 Disney film *Frozen* depicts the archetypal tale of hiding and shrinking. In the story, the protagonist Elsa possesses the magic power of turning everything into ice. When she was little and had not learned to master her power, she accidentally injured her sister Anna. Then, in the name of protection, their parents taught Elsa to hide her power to stay safe. They erased her sister's memory, pretending that Elsa's power did not exist. They shut Elsa off from the world and told her to 'conceal it, don't feel it, don't let it show'. Elsa no longer felt able to laugh and play with a carefree spirit. She was ashamed of who she was and believed that allowing her true self to be seen meant she would either be rejected or that she would hurt someone.

Like Elsa, you might have learned to become frightened of your gifts. From an early age, emotionally intense individuals are naturally trusting, loving and giving; they have the tendency to experience and express love and passion fiercely and intensely, often before they have learned to manage their energies. Yet their openness can almost seem intimidating to others. As they are incredibly perceptive, their intolerance for lies and phoniness means they often expose the most inconvenient truth in any given situation. This often sets them up to be the scapegoat in the group, sometimes even in their family. Elsa's story touches us because she reminds us of the isolation and fear we feel when we reject ourselves to avoid being seen as too weird or different. Like Elsa, perhaps you went through many dark nights when you were afraid of what lay within you.

The first step to awakening from the unconscious trance of hiding is to have an awareness that it is happening and to look squarely at its origins. Let's review some psychological factors that may have kept you hiding and shrinking.

## NEEDING TO FEEL SAFE

Combining your gifted perception with an intense sense of justice and an unwavering passion for life, it is inevitable that you ask the dangerous questions. Driven by your natural curiosity and drive for excellence, you test the boundaries of conformity. This makes you a natural visionary, but like all visionaries across history, you might be fiercely attacked and rejected. Since most people who live within their comfort zone dread change, the fact that you challenge the status quo makes others feel threatened.

In a world of compliance, bureaucracy and power play, you can find yourself being oppressed and alienated. Many gifted individuals find themselves perceived as a threat that needs to be eliminated. From school to the workplace, social reactions towards them are demeaning and hostile. Your astuteness amplifies your fear, as you can pick up the most subtle cues of attacks and ridicule in any given social situation. As a result, your fear system becomes chronically activated, and you become haunted by the fear of being ostracized. To survive socially and to self-preserve, you may then decide at some point in your life to hide your capabilities to avoid being seen as a threat to others.

## THE DEEP YEARNING TO BELONG

The desire to belong to a group is a part of human nature. However, due to your unusual perceptivity and ultra-sensitivity, you may have always felt as if you were on the outside looking in.

Many gifted and emotionally sensitive individuals feel an intense inner conflict: they want to show up in the world as their real self, yet they do not want to sacrifice their belongingness. The existential tension of wanting to be authentic while still being part of a group is heightened most strongly around adolescence, often creating strong internal conflicts that persist into adulthood. As in the story of 'The Ugly Duckling', though you were born a swan, you might have tried your whole life trying to fit in as a duckling. You may soon discover that hiding is not a sustainable strategy: if you adopt a false self and pretend to be something that you are not, even if that facade is accepted, deep down you will still feel imperfect and unlovable. Eventually, you would no longer be able to suppress the cry from your most passionate, daring and authentic self.

## 'What if I am crazy?'

Due to their perceptivity and ability to rapidly assimilate information from their surroundings, many empathically gifted people have an unerring instinct about people and events. You may have a sense of knowing when something is about to happen, and have insights into other people's inner worlds. For instance, you can often tell if someone is telling the truth or hiding something. You may also have vivid dreams or other exceptional metaphysical encounters. However, these experiences might have worried or frightened you because we live in an intellectually dominated world that demonizes non-mainstream understanding of consciousness.

The word 'psychic' is often used to describe someone who can relate to what is lying outside the world of physical science or knowledge, and is responsive to non-physical or magical forces and effects. Most ultra-empathic individuals have a degree of sensitivity, perception and knowledge that is beyond the standard. Sadly, doctrines of all kinds have taught us to fear what we cannot objectively measure. In fact, most of the world denies the presence of any emotional and energetic transfer. As a result, rather than owning this natural ability, you might have become afraid of it. You would rather deny your power than be seen as crazy.

## SEPARATION ANXIETY AND SURVIVOR GUILT

Most of us are not aware of the unconscious fears and motives that hold us back from expressing our true self. A psychological analysis carried out in 1997 by Shilkret and Nigrosh with a group of talented college women revealed two unconscious inhibitors of their performance and well-being: separation anxiety and survivor guilt.

Separation anxiety is the belief that your freedom is threatening or dangerous to the well-being of your loved ones. Your fear may be that what you see and know will separate you from those close to you.

Survivor guilt, in this context, refers to the potential feeling of remorse over being able to know and see what others in your family don't, or that you feel undeserving of the opportunities you've had that have not been accessible to them. When, as a child, you showed your outstanding ability to process and gather information or to generate ideas, your family might have tried to shut you down so that you didn't outshine your brothers and sisters. Or, maybe you were prevented from telling the truth so as to save face for the family. Perhaps your upbringing and culture have said it is selfish to reveal your abilities. Many years of social conditioning, particularly among collectivist cultures (which emphasize the needs of the group as a whole over the needs of each individual, and promote values such as selflessness and harmony), claims that you have to consider others' feelings and thoughts before you express yourself.

Although it may seem irrational on the surface, subconsciously you believe that stepping out of the traditional cultural values and doctrines that you have been brought up with implies betrayal; you may think that if you were to escape from the cultural limits, you would be leaving other people behind.

The urge to hide and shrink in the name of protecting their families is particularly common amongst gifted women. Whether because of nature or nurture, women tend to value relationships more highly and take others' perspectives into account. Despite societal changes, many women still feel that they have to choose between relationships and making their mark in the world. Many have internalized the message that they can be either competent or nurturing, but not both. Even when a gifted woman sees that it is irrational to underachieve, she may continue to do so if deep down she believes that success will result in a failure in the realm of relationships and intimacy. As Marianne Williamson says in her work *A Woman's Worth* (1993): 'Women are still in emotional bondage as long as we need to worry that we might have to make a choice between being heard and being loved.'

Going back to the movie *Frozen*, one of the most memorable scenes is when Elsa sings 'Let It Go' on the mountain top. As she stomps her feet on the ground, she fully manifests her power for the first time in years. We are empowered as we hear: 'I am never going back... It's time to see what I can do. Here I am, and here I stay!' We who know the sorrow of hiding are touched, because the song echoes our ultimate yearning as human beings to be seen, heard and accepted for who we are. Ultimately, *Frozen* is a story of 'un-freezing', where the heroine learns to accept her true self and to show her real power. Embedded in the tale is an important message for all exceptional individuals who do not fit nicely into society's mould: you do not have to sacrifice the truth of who you are, to be loved. Hiding your true self to fit in will paradoxically make you feel more alone and separated from the rest of the world. Most importantly, by playing small you are depriving the world of your gifts, and that serves absolutely no one. The goal is to find the place where your gifts are celebrated, rather than tolerated and, ultimately, you do not have to choose between power and love, or between freedom and connection. You can have both. The biggest tragedy is that if you pretend to be less capable than you actually are, you will eventually forget about your real potential, and you will disappear into the crowd.

# Reflection prompts: have you been hiding and shrinking?

Find a time and space to be with your journal. Sitting comfortably, bring your awareness to your breathing. Then ask yourself the following questions:

1 Reviewing my life and the environment I grew up in, from school to home, did I notice any 'Tall Poppy Syndrome', 'Crab-in-the-Bucket' mentality, or 'Law of Jante' in operation? How has this changed the way I present or conduct myself in group situations?

2 What have I not said, or done, to fit in and to not be seen as 'weird'?

3 Do I suffer from 'Imposter Syndrome' – feeling like a fraud on the inside?

4 Do I struggle with receiving compliments, or only attribute my achievements to luck or external assistance?

5 How have I changed as I learned to restrict myself in life, and what would my youngest, most unrestricted self think of me now?

6 How have hiding and shrinking served to keep me safe?

7 How have hiding and shrinking also kept me playing it small, or stopped me from fulfilling my potential?

8 Is there, or was there, anyone in my life that I feel I can't or shouldn't shine around?

9 Who might I be trying to help feel better by playing it small?

10 Who might not like it if I were to become outrageously successful?

11 What would I say or do if it was completely safe to do so?

Simply being aware of the factors and old beliefs that are holding you back is the first step towards liberation. In later chapters, we will look further into the dilemma of authenticity versus safety, and how to be rid of the beliefs that no longer keep you safe, and only keep you down.

# In your mind

# The shame of being 'too much'

Many emotionally sensitive people have accumulated experiences of being misunderstood and marginalized. When your attempts to be your spontaneous, natural self are rejected, you feel shame. After a while, you might internalize the message that something is wrong with you. Being different can be lonely, but the real suffering lies in the feeling that you, as a person, are fundamentally 'not okay'.

When shame becomes toxic and chronic, it takes over your entire sense of self. A person who has been chronically shamed feels it is about 'who they are' rather than about an action they did. Internalized chronic shame tells you you are inherently bad and totally flawed as a person; it is not just a feeling, but a sense of identity, an all-encompassing state of being.

Chronic shame is debilitating and paralysing. You may be hyper-vigilant and worry-prone because you do not believe that you have the right to make mistakes. When you do, you may feel that you 'are' the mistakes. You can easily slip into seeing yourself as disgusting, ugly, stupid or defective. Much of what we know as anxiety and panic stems from shame. For instance, underlying social anxiety is the fear of feeling embarrassed or humiliated by other people, which is fuelled by a deep sense of defectiveness; a worry that the 'defective self' will be found out.

When triggered by situations in life where you feel exposed, humiliated, embarrassed, or that you are 'too much', you may experience a visceral 'shame attack' – your body goes into shock, your heart rate goes up, and your palms start to sweat. After the initial shock, shame then morphs into a state of helplessness and despair. You collapse, both externally and internally. You may feel that all the blood is being drained out of you and that you have to curl up, put your head down, and avoid looking anyone in the eye. Many people describe the experience of a shame attack as 'an earthquake', or 'as if the rug was pulled from under my feet'. Afterwards, you feel raw and exposed, as if you are walking around with no skin. In more extreme cases, self-loathing and helplessness can lead to suicidal thoughts and self-harming behaviours.

Another way shame shows up is as a harsh inner critic – an internal voice that says: 'You are no good'; 'Others don't like you'; 'You'll never be able to find true love and belonging'. Shame says: 'Nothing you do is good enough'; 'There is something fundamentally wrong with you'; 'You are bad and dangerous'. It can even turn into a terrifyingly destructive voice that says you don't deserve a place in this world.

Shame is the biggest factor holding you back from authentic living. Having internalized shame, you may try to hide your true self from yourself. When the most passionate, creative and spontaneous part of you goes into hiding, it becomes alienated. In essence, you are trying to forget about part of your truth, by denying your feelings, needs and drives. To survive, you may present a 'false self' to the world and hide your real self. As you do this, it becomes harder and harder for you to believe that your real self is acceptable. If you spend your life trying to please others with a mask on, you will eventually lose faith in the idea that your authentic self is lovable. The vicious cycle perpetuates itself. This results in further withdrawal, passivity and inaction.

Shame also blocks your creative potential. When you constantly scrutinize, monitor and limit yourself, there remains little space for playfulness, spontaneity and joy. You procrastinate because you feel that you must do things perfectly or not at all. Or, you feel too fatigued to do anything, as your energy is used up defending your injured self from further shame attacks. As you stop freely expressing yourself, you feel more and more cut off from your natural vitality, and your creativity becomes stifled.

However, you will not be able to suppress your yearnings for expression for very long. Even after being shunned and shut down, the voice of your authentic self is undeniable and must, inevitably, come out. Your low-grade depression and emptiness are the grief at losing your most daring and passionate self. The more you resist it, the more life presents with you the wake-up call. You may find yourself suddenly facing unexpected life events that violently tear down the fabric of your life. Serious illness, accidents and spiritual crises can all serve as turning points, leaving you with no choice but to face your emotional baggage. Other wake-up calls take a more subtle and gradual form: perhaps you can no longer deny how tired and restless you feel in a dead-end job, career or relationship. Your body and psyche may be complaining to you by way of physical illness or mental breakdown.

Because of how horribly disempowering and unpleasant shame feels, we rarely allow ourselves to stay with it. Our default is to dissociate and evade. We may get emotionally numb, or try to distract ourselves with pleasure, compulsive behaviours or overachieving. Or we may cover it up with rage, or inflated pride. None of these strategies offers lasting solutions. The more we evade it, the more shame runs our lives. Getting to know shame – without further blaming yourself for having it – is an essential first step. Coming out of chronic shame may take more than a few steps. However, your body and mind naturally want to heal and move towards integration. With the right tools, you can grow and recover from even the most painful shaming experience.

To recap, here is a list of some of the signs that point to chronic shame:

▶ You live with a constant feeling of inadequacy. Deep down, you believe that you are somehow defective, flawed, inferior and unlovable.

▶ When triggered, the shameful feelings are experienced to a great intensity and last for an extended period.

▶ Your shameful feelings can quickly spiral into more severe panic or depression.

▶ You experience extreme anxiety about being around other people, especially those you perceive as 'seeing through' you or as 'better than you'.

▶ You avoid activities or opportunities that may cause shame. For example, you may reject a job promotion because of the potential exposure.

▶ To avoid rejection, you would rather isolate yourself than to risk connecting to other people.

▶ You devalue yourself before others do, or leave a relationship before others can.

▶ You react very strongly to criticism, either with rage or intense self-loathing.

▶ Despite your outward achievements, you have a feeling that you are a fraud, and that others will reject you once they get to know the 'real you'.

## Exercise: knowing your shame

1  Close your eyes, hang your head down and allow your body to slouch. Now, search in your memory bank for a time during your childhood when you felt shamed by either an authority figure or your peers. It can be any time when you remember being told in so many words that you were wrong, lacking or defective in some way. Much of shame is about failing to meet other people's expectations – in a way, we have simply internalized the values of those who attempted to shame us.

2  In your mind's eye, look around you. How old were you? Where were you? What was happening? Did the sense of shame come from an outside person, or a harsh internal judgement from yourself, or both?

3  Notice your immediate, visceral reactions to shame.
Shame tends to create a sense of shrinkage. Did you tighten your body? Did you feel the heat in your head and face? Perhaps your mind drew a blank? Did you lose time or memory for a period?

4  Recall how you have chosen to deal with this sense of shame. What happened after the incident? Did you erupt in rage, fight back, or did you collapse and withdraw?

5  Now, with the feeling of shame still lingering within you, recall a recent time where you felt shame. It can be big or small, at home or work – any time you had a similar emotional experience to when you were shamed as a child. Again, look around you. Where were you? What was happening?

6  Now, notice how you dealt with shame as an adult. Did you adopt the same strategy? Did you feel anger, or a desire to retaliate? Or perhaps you found yourself wanting to withdraw from the world? Did you resort to escapist behaviours such as excessive eating or drinking? Sometimes, without knowing it, we may use less obvious strategies, such as compulsive controlling behaviours or people-pleasing as a way of coping with chronic shame.

# Emotional storms and being out of control

A common emotional difficulty faced by emotionally intense people is the feeling of being out of control. Others may have described you as being 'emotionally unstable', because of the velocity and intensity of your feelings, and how rapidly they shift from one to another. However, feeling out of control is more than just a mood change. It is as if there are different personalities inside of you, each with their own mannerisms, feelings and character. You may feel that you go from your 'normal' mode one minute to a different mode the next, in which you feel and act like a completely different person. For instance, you can have an 'angry mode', a 'sad mode' and a 'shut-down mode'. Perhaps one moment you are impulsive, the next moment you are numb and detached. When you are in a destructive mode, the other healthier, more resourceful parts of you seem to vanish, and you are not able to bring yourself back to calm. As a result, you find yourself doing things you don't want to do, feeling things you don't want to feel, or saying things that you don't want to say. What makes it even more challenging is that sometimes the triggers for your emotional flips are not known to you. You may simply 'wake up feeling bad' without knowing why.

### THE POWER OF OUR MEMORIES

Let's look at how theories in the field of cognitive psychology and neuroscience explain these sudden and drastic shifts in your feelings and behaviours.

Every day, we absorb information from the outside world through our five senses. As adults, we automatically connect the day-to-day information coming our way with what is already in our system to make sense of what is going on. For instance, right now you are linking up the words you are reading to your knowledge of English grammar, vocabulary and syntax that are stored in your memory network. In the same way, your memories are the basis of your current perception, and how you respond to people and events in your life is, to a great extent, based on your past experiences.

In psychology, the relationship between conscious and unconscious memories can be represented as an iceberg, with the majority of the mind remaining buried and unconscious. Everything that has ever happened to you has been recorded in your memory, even if you do not consciously recall it. Your current attitudes, emotions and sensations are not merely reactions to a current event but are also manifestations of physiologically stored information in your memory.

According to the Adaptive Information Processing Model (Shapiro, 2007), our brain has a processing system that is naturally geared towards integration and healing. When uninterrupted, it can link up useful and restorative memories with the difficult ones, to help us maintain a certain degree of emotional equilibrium.

However, if we experienced an unusually painful or traumatic situation that overwhelmed us, such as being repeatedly humiliated or shamed as a child, the adaptive processing would be disrupted.

During the first six years of life, we live in what is called a Delta Theta brainwave state. Before we are able to think rationally or to express ourselves, all our experiences – good, bad and ugly – are recorded through the reasoning level of a child. This is particularly problematic because the memory of the original distressing situation will be stored in the brain in its original form, with the visceral reactions and logical reasoning of a child's mind. For instance, even when nothing objectively disastrous had happened, if as a five-year-old we had felt unloved or rejected by the world, that would be how the memory remains in us – with all the helplessness, hopelessness and fear of a five-year-old. The distressing incident got stored in our mind in a way that was 'frozen in time', and became a stand-alone piece of information, disconnected to the other parts of our memory network. In other words, we remain 'stuck' because that piece of traumatic experience is stored in the memory in isolation, unintegrated within the newer, more useful and adaptive information (e.g. 'I am an adult now, and I am resourceful') that promotes healing. Even if we do not consciously remember them, these dysfunctionally held pieces of information are the driving force behind our uncontrollable feelings and behaviours.

## WHAT DOES ALL THIS MEAN TO YOU IN THE PRESENT DAY?

For traumatized emotionally intense and sensitive children, the trauma was often not one-off, but chronic and relational. For example, you may have experienced parental coldness, inconsistencies or 'invisible' abuse, compounded with being bullied and misunderstood in school. If there were too many of these traumatic experiences, your memories would be dissociated into fragments.

Since your subconscious mind works by association, without your conscious awareness, seemingly random imagery and sensory associations can set off your painful memories. Sometimes it is so subtle and rapid that your reasoning mind is not able to catch up or make sense of it.

Whenever something occurs that the brain associates with your original upset, the memory of that bad experience is re-activated. You may suddenly feel drastically different, have certain intrusive thoughts, or act in a certain way. When you have a 'mood flip', as if you suddenly switch from being a rational adult into a tantrum-throwing child, you are re-living the trauma at the level of that of a child. As a result, you may lash out at your partner, have inexplicable rage, or engage in addictive or self-sabotaging behaviour without knowing why.

We have little control over these episodes of collapse or outbursts because whenever our trauma memories are re-activated, the conscious, logical, thinking mind is bypassed. This is a mechanism that is hardwired to protect us: since there is a perceived threat, our fight-or-flight system kicks in and takes over for the purpose of survival or protection, and it is given priority over reasoning and logic. While the image of the event may not return visually, as it often would if you had post traumatic stress disorder, your emotional flashback may show up in other ways such as negative self-talk, a knot in your stomach, tightness in the chest, or a flood of fear, shame and powerlessness.

The reason we cannot quickly identify the real cause of our reactions is that we may be totally unaware of the stimulus that caused them. The anger, sorrow and pain that are running the show now might be from unprocessed memories from many years ago. However, it is useful to know that when our reaction seems 'illogical' or 'disproportionate', the real stimulus is almost always a memory. The worst is in the past.

## Exercise: working with triggers

A trigger is something that reminds you of an unresolved experience, thus evoking an array of unpleasant emotions. Triggers can be a person, an object, a situation, a type of interaction, a location or even a time of day. When you are triggered, you react with the same level of emotional charge as during the original situation. So, if the original painful event happened when you were five, you might find yourself suddenly behaving like a five-year-old again. Because the past event is locked away in some part of your memory bank, you will continue to be triggered as long as the dissociative parts of yourself remain stuck in trauma-time.

1 Identify a time when you were triggered. You know that you were triggered when one or more of the following happens:
   a Your reaction to the present-day situation seemed more intense than was warranted.
   b You felt like a child or teenager rather than an adult.
   c You lost control of what you said or did.
   d You felt completely out of control as if someone else was running your life.
   e You were not able to step back and reflect.
   f You might have become enraged, or found yourself collapsing in shame.
2 Where were you, what were you doing and who were you with when you were triggered?
3 Describe what triggered you – what did you see, hear, perceive?
4 What were the thoughts and feelings that came to you when you were triggered? Recall the physical sensations too. Some examples may be intense fear, panic, pain, nausea, or feeling like you were out of your body.
5 Approximately how old did you feel?
6 Many triggers are social and situational – were you triggered by another person? Or a group situation? Sometimes you can recognize the link between a trigger and your experience, but sometimes you have no memory of the original event and cannot make sense of the

connection. In either case, you can still benefit from careful reflection and work on reducing the severity and frequency of this happening. With practice, the reaction to your emotional triggers could subside, but they may never go away. The best you can do is to quickly identify when an emotion is triggered and then choose what to say or do next.

7 Describe any options you had in retrospect, but did not realize at the time. If you were to anticipate this trigger in the future, how might you prepare for it? What inner resources might you call upon? For example, can you assertively ask for what you need, or assert your position, rather than feeling deprived or victimized? Or, do you have the capacity to let go of this feeling for now?

8 Try to mentally rehearse a similar situation in the future. Bring up as vivid a scenario as possible, and imagine yourself dealing with it in a different way. Choose what you want to feel and what you want to do.

## Feeling empty and numb

'I am emotionally intense, but mostly I feel nothing, empty, detached from reality and those around me…'

Though it sounds paradoxical at first, many emotionally intense and sensitive people struggle with 'emotional numbness', a kind of internal deadness or emptiness that permeates their whole being and strips them of the joy and fullness that life has to offer.

At first glance, it seems counter-intuitive that emotional numbness could exist at the same time with emotional intensity, but an understanding of how the human mind works sheds light on the connection. Emotional numbness finds its origin in a part of our personal history that is too painful to reach. It is in our human nature to defend against pain. Once we have experienced a physically or emotionally painful situation, such as being betrayed or intruded upon, we will focus all our attention on preventing it happening again. In the face of physical, emotional or relational traumatic experiences, human beings have three responses: fight, flight or freeze. If disconnecting with others to avoid getting hurt is 'fleeing', then numbing out our emotions altogether is 'freezing'. When faced with extreme situations such as rejection, abandonment or shame, our body and psyche to go into a 'numbing mode' as part of that freezing response. In fact, dissociation is built into our system to protect us: it comes from our animal instincts to enable us to survive the most unimaginably difficult circumstances. When things overwhelm us, disconnecting might be the only way that we can preserve our sanity or save our life.

However, this protective reflex sometimes remains for much longer after the actual danger has passed. Emotional numbing tends not to be a conscious choice; you may not even be aware of the pattern building until after it becomes your 'normal' way of functioning. Initially, emotional disconnection offers a sense of pseudo-equanimity, a steady state of pleasantness, which also allows you to present a socially acceptable persona. You may feel that you can function normally – get up in the morning, get dressed, go to work. But eventually, it becomes deadening. This protective shield can seem useful at first: you will feel that the pain has gone away and that you can 'get on with life', perhaps even with confidence. Although the pattern started off as a way of protecting yourself from others, it can eventually morph into your hiding from yourself or denying your needs altogether.

Emotional numbness, or detachment, is experienced differently by different people: you may feel a lingering sense of boredom and emptiness, that you are not able to show or feel any emotion. You may lose the ability to respond to events with the usual joy or sadness, or you struggle to connect with others in a deep and meaningful way. In psychology, the term 'affect phobia' is used to describe the tendency for some people to avoid feelings that they believe are intolerable. As a result, they become emotionally detached and experience life in a 'dissociated' or 'depersonalized' way. The way your shield works can be likened to what psychologist Jeffrey Young calls the 'detached protector mode'. Signs and symptoms of the mode include 'depersonalization, emptiness, boredom, substance abuse, bingeing, self-mutilation, psychosomatic complaints, "blankness", or [adopting] a cynical, aloof or pessimistic stance to avoid investing in people or activities' (Young, 2003).

### THE PAIN AND DANGER OF FREEZING UP
Though it may seem like a decent solution for emotional survival, detaching from pain carries many downsides. For one,

suppressed emotions tend to accumulate in your system, leaving you with a calm facade that conceals the real psychic wounds: anger, both expressed and repressed; longing for what might have been; distress over past betrayal; or grief over relationships that ended too soon. With so much hidden within, you may feel particularly sensitive and irritable. It may take only minor events for you to reach your 'boiling point', where you may be caught off-guard by emotional outbursts that seem to come out of nowhere.

If you feel cut off from the entirety of your being, you may do certain things that are not in line with your true will. For instance, if your basic needs for comfort and safety are not met, you may resort to self-soothing by over-eating, over-spending, or engaging in other impulsive behaviours.

When you turn away from feeling bad emotions, you turn away from feeling good emotions too. You may become an observer of life, watching it go by without being 'in' it. Some people may even experience memory loss, as they do not remember much of their life – even looking at old pictures of themselves can seem surreal. Life's pain may seem dampened, but you will not feel the full extent of positive emotions either: love, joy and friendship. Although things may seem fine on the outside, you may feel overcome by a wave of sadness or loneliness. Any reminder of life's finiteness can bring on painful existential anxiety and guilt. This is because even though part of you insists on freezing up, there is something deep down in you that cannot help but remind you that you are missing out on life.

Ultimately, you know that the strategy of locking your heart away is no longer working and that to choose to live this life fully is to allow your heart to melt, blossom and ache, all at the same time. Inside of you is a wildly spontaneous, innocent and playful child. Deep down, you long to engage in life fully, to feel completely safe in the presence of others, and to love without holding back, as that is the call from your nature.

The path outlined in later chapters will guide you through the construction of emotional skills and resilience so that you can begin to feel safe enough to dip your feet into the deep waters of feeling. We will start with small strategies, such as learning to label emotions and self-regulate. Once you begin to develop a degree of emotional capacity, the 'thawing' process will naturally follow. At that point, you will have re-opened the door to experience life's joy, abundance and aliveness – things that a hidden part of you has long been yearning for.

## Exercise: working with your shield

### 1 Relinquishing any blame and shame

The first step to working with your emotional numbness is to relinquish any shame or self-criticism attached to it. On top of the pain of feeling empty, you may have accumulated many experiences of being shamed in relationships and the conflicts associated with that. For instance, your intimate partner may have accused you of being cold, defensive or distanced when they needed affection from you. However, it is important to remember that your numbness grew out of a place of pain and tenderness, and was nothing but a desperate attempt to survive. Shaming or punishing yourself for becoming numb in the first place will only reinforce the defensive pattern.

### 2 Acknowledging the sadness

Once you have put away your harsh internal critic, you are ready to approach your numbness from a place of compassion. This is important because when you first acknowledge the extent to which your numbness has held you back from joy, you will hit a wave of sadness. This is grief over the fact that you have been out of touch with yourself and your true nature all this time. Instead of bypassing your sadness, set an intention to move closer to it, feel into it, so it can be digested, rather than suppressed.

### 3 Examining the shield

Now, you are ready to look carefully at your numbness. Use your imagination, and reflect on the following questions:

* If your emotional numbness is a wall, or a shield, how thick is it?
* What kind of material is it made of? Metal, wood or plastic? How dense or heavy is it?
* When you touch into your wall/shield, does it feel warm, or cold?
* Does it change according to your life circumstances or energy levels, or does it remain stuck and static?
* If your wall/shield has a voice, what is it saying?

## 4 Thanking and transforming the numbness

Keep approaching your shield, until you reach the tender wounds that lie beneath it. Breathe gently and deeply through this process. Only then, you may wish to say: 'Thank you for protecting me all these years. I would not have survived without you. However, I am stronger now, and I no longer need you.'

Your goal here is not to get rid of the shield but to befriend it and get to know it, so it no longer runs the show. We do not expect things to change overnight, and you may have to repeat the process of approaching it and examining it again and again.

The next time you find yourself using the shield to defend against emotions, or when you feel numb where you want to feel alive and present, you will be more aware, and your numbness will no longer be an unconscious, destructive force. Your emotional shield aims to protect, and you may choose to use it, or not. But the power remains in you.

# Part 3

## From healing to thriving

So far, we have looked at some of the difficulties and challenges that the emotionally intense commonly face. In the third part of this book, I will guide you through a series of reflection exercises and practice, where our goal is to move from healing to thriving.

We will begin by healing the wounds left by early trauma and negative experiences. When we are carrying with us old emotional baggage, painful memories, familiar patterns and a negative mindset, we cannot bypass this necessary step. However, ultimately, you do not want just to survive. You want to THRIVE. Beyond healing, you want to gain inner strength, be true to yourself and tap into your most profound potential.

We will look at how to stay open to your emotions, to the unpredictability of life, and to the painful events and challenging people in the world. We will also examine what it means to live an authentic life, how to express yourself, find a sense of belonging in the world, circumvent toxic relationship patterns and break through creative blockages.

In Chapter 8 we will focus on acknowledging the unmet needs in your past and letting go of any lingering resentment. We will also look at your relationship with your family and how to deal with reactions and emotions in you that they may trigger. Chapter 9 is about finding your internal sense of safety, learning how to deal with your intense emotions without becoming either overwhelmed or detached, and accepting that life doesn't always turn out the way you want it to. In Chapter 10 we will explore the meaning of `authenticity' and look at how to let go of who you think you should be and accept yourself as you are. This chapter is also about optimizing your creativity and productivity, and building a life around your values. Chapter 11 is all about your relationships with other people: being aware of and preserving your emotional boundaries; understanding negative social dynamics and passive-aggression; reflecting on what you see in others to further your own personal growth; and coming to regard relationships as enriching rather than tiring or threatening. In Chapter 12 we look at intimate relationships: recognizing compromised and dysfunctional relationship patterns; developing nurturing relationships in which you are celebrated, not merely tolerated; having the courage to love without holding back; and opening yourself up to your emotions. Finally, in Chapter 13, we'll explore how to maximize your creative potential.

Don't be discouraged if some of the ideas explored seem unreachable to you right now. Emotional healing and self-actualizing are lifelong paths that each of us can progress along with commitment and continuous practice. Although the chapters are presented in a linear sequence, you may find yourself going back and forth through them. Please follow your instincts, feel free to take on board only what chimes with you and leave the rest behind.

# Healing old wounds

# Telling the truth

The first step towards emotional healing is to come face to face with the truth. 'Truth' here does not mean universal truth, but your subjective reality. Your individual story is your unique, visceral and historical blueprint.

Emotions related to loss – such as sadness, neediness and vulnerability – are painful to bear, and our default reaction is often to push them away. If parts of your childhood experience have been painful, it could be that those parts of your story have lain dormant in your subconscious mind as repressed, denied, suppressed or dissociated content that has bypassed your conscious mind.

In our modern world of self-help and positive psychology, we are advised to think or will ourselves to health, to refuse to identify with the role of the victim and to refrain from blaming others. However, this does not mean we should deny ourselves the full expression of our anger and hurt or to rush towards forgiveness. To heal, we need to consciously acknowledge our stories: our real chronicles, stored inside our bodies at a cellular, emotional level. As we do this, we can free up the energy spent on repression, and make space for vitality and joy.

Unlike shock trauma or physical abuse, psychological injuries are invisible and often unacknowledged. As a child, perhaps you were forced to silence yourself at times, because expressions of needs and wants were forbidden or even dangerous. Even as an adult, you may have developed the habit of 'talking around' or simply 'talking about' your story, rather than truly allowing yourself to experience any feelings directly. In doing so, however, you are keeping a part of your story shame-bound and locked away. There is now plenty of scientific evidence which suggests that denial of feelings has a detrimental impact on mental and physical health. When you deny your truest feelings, the internal conflict created stresses your biological system, which may then show itself in the form of aches and pains, allergies, and chronic physical and mental fatigue.

You initially learned to disguise your emotional pain to protect yourself. Your young mind may not have had the support or resources necessary to deal with a reality too cruel to bear. Or maybe you were in a volatile and chaotic environment with no space to safely express yourself. Uncovering what lies underneath your past can seem threatening, but false tranquillity upheld by a facade of 'okay-ness' is fragile and short-lived. In the end, self-deception is toxic; unmourned pains and unspoken words can only lie dormant for so long. Although initially uncomfortable, the process of delving deep into your past may provide significant release from the burden that your emotional body has been carrying all along.

## BEING WITNESSED

Pain is most insidious when kept secret. In order to release your burden and have your deprived inner child – finally – fully seen and heard, it can be helpful to summon the aid of another person. Psychologist Alice Miller spoke of the importance of having an 'Enlightened Witness': someone capable of helping you to recognize the injustices or pain you have suffered and to provide a space in which to tell your story (Miller, 2008).

If you have had to be self-reliant all your life, you may find it tough to trust others. But there is something fundamentally and uniquely healing about having another bear witness to your story – something that cannot be easily replaced by self-help strategies. The goal of telling your story is for you to experience the profound healing effect of having your truth seen, heard and believed. If you have a tendency to detach from your feelings, then having someone witness your story will be a huge step towards integration.

To make this process a safe one, you must ensure that your witness does not analyse or invalidate you. They must not be there to defend any people, events or organizations, including institutions such as the Church. In the delicate moment of telling your story, it is essential that they do not patronize you or give you advice.

If you cannot identify people in your inner circle who can be objective and non-judgemental, you may consider seeking out professional help. However, be mindful that counsellors and therapists are people too, and are not immune to internalizing society's unconscious prejudices. If they bring their own cultural and religious baggage, you may come away feeling more wounded than before. You certainly do not want a replay of your earlier relationships, in which your intuitiveness and progressive thinking becomes a threat. The key is to keep looking and trust your intuition in identifying your trusted other.

Once you have identified your trusted witness and clearly established that their task is simply to listen to your story with no agenda, you may start telling the story of what it has been like to grow up as an emotionally intense person in an insensitive world. See if you can recount your story in first-person, rather than third-person narration. When telling your truth, look for detailed images, memories and examples: try to give people in your story names (say 'Dr Smith', rather than 'my doctor'), and be as honest and specific as possible.

Your witness can help you to be aware of any deviation from telling your story in a way that feels 'real', such as when you narrate as if it is someone else's story. They can also help you notice the discrepancies between what you say you are feeling and what your body is expressing. For instance, you may be hunching over, crossing your fingers, while saying 'I have been fine and happy all along'.

Although it can be painful, this is an essential first step to healing the wounds that have been caused by being misunderstood, neglected, scapegoated or insufficiently nurtured. Expressing your feelings to someone who will honour them grants you the opportunity to reverse the effects of being silenced – today you no longer need anyone's permission to express how you feel.

If you cannot find someone or if it is not easy for you to tell someone, then see if you can draw or write your story down. You can identify someone with whom it is safe to share it at a later time.

**Reflection prompts:** what are my truths?

Find a time and space to be with your journal. Sitting comfortably, bring your awareness to your breathing. Then reflect on the following:

1 Notice how you relate to the painful parts of your past. Do you have a tendency to minimize your negative feelings and judgements? Do you have a habit of talking about yourself in the third-person to distance yourself from your experiences? Do you hit a blank when you try to recall childhood memories?

2 Allow yourself to be honest: what was it like to grow up as a sensitive person in an insensitive household? Who did you turn to when you felt sad and lonely? How did it feel to not have a sense of shared reality with those around you? Was it really 'okay' to have to be the little adult at home, rather than being able to lean on your caregivers?

3 As you reflect on these questions, notice the discrepancy between what you say and how you feel on the inside. Your body does not lie: look at your energy level and your physical aches and pains. Despite how you think you 'should' feel, your body reveals your true struggle. When you bring up, for instance, a particular scenario, does your breathing become faster? Do you feel heat anywhere inside you? Do you feel a knot in your stomach or tension in your shoulders? Cultivating this kind of emotional awareness involves not just thinking about your feelings, but also feeling them in gentle awareness. In the process of healing, it is crucial that you link your emotions with some bodily sensations. Intellectualizing itself does not heal: your physical and emotional selves must also be activated for change to occur.

# Letting go of 'what might have been'

After the courageous step of acknowledging your story and your truth, the next step towards healing any kind of emotional wounds is grieving.

When we think of loss and grief we often think about bereavement, or traumatic events such as sickness and war. There is, however, another kind of 'ambiguous loss' that is often overlooked: the loss of a childhood. If you were brought up in a hostile social environment, where there was neglect, rejection or criticism, or where your young heart was overwhelmed with not only hurt and anger but also deep despair and disappointment, you have lost your innocence too soon.

Grief arises in response to never having had something. In essence you are grieving for a fantasy, a life you never had. The yearning for 'what might have been' has now left a void in your heart. You may not be able to name the feeling as grief, but experience it as a sense of emptiness, or perhaps a perpetual homesickness, of never feeling a sense of belonging or safety in the world. Mourning the loss of the childhood you never had can be more difficult than losing someone, and you may swing between denial, anger, disbelief and depression before you can reach acceptance.

Because grieving involves pain, our default position is to run away. This is usually unconscious, but we would do anything just to avoid the deep pain of not having had the childhood that we always wanted. Yet the refusal to grieve is precisely what causes sickness in the heart. Sadness is there to help you release that which no longer serves you, and allowing it to go through you will restore a sense of flow in your life. Psychologists and therapists know this: depression is not caused by sadness itself but, paradoxically, the resistance to being sad and allowing the emotions to go through you. When you reject sadness and mourning, your healing flow will be obstructed by your unmet needs, your unexpressed rage, and your unshed tears. Ultimately, what you push away haunts you the most.

To make matters worse, in order to avoid further losses and disappointments, many wounded sensitive people have become detached from passion, love and human relationships. You may also have turned to sensation seeking and emotion-numbing behaviours such as comfort eating, excessive drinking, or self-medicating in order to mask your deep longing for love, safety and belonging.

To move forward, you can mourn the 'normal childhood' that you never had. Rather than suppressing it, and have it turning into unconscious and toxic bitterness, you can acknowledge the sadness, and mourn what needs to be mourned.

Even if they had the best intentions, your parents' limited capacities might have meant that they were not able to protect you from the abrasive effects of bullying, to celebrate your gifts, honour your intuition, or cherish your sensitivities. You may need to mourn the unfortunate truth that when you were growing up a gifted child, few or no adults were strong or capable enough for you to lean on; there was no one there who was able to support you, protect you or guide you. Without a strong role model or guardian, you were not acknowledged for your light, and so did not learn how to value yourself. On the other hand, if you were bullied by your peers, it is natural for you to feel sad and angry. It was extremely painful for your younger self that your intensity and vitality were so hugely misunderstood and this alienated you from those around you.

In grieving, you allow your fantasies and idealizations to die off, just like the butterfly that sheds its cocoon. Although you may never completely stop feeling sad for your lost childhood, the intensity of your pain and anger will gradually cease. The pains and insults were real, but these wounds are only toxic if they remain invisible. Once you have exposed them and acknowledged them for what they are, they gradually cease to have power over you. In truth, grief is the best medicine for your pain; it is a poignant and sacred process that offers true liberation in the end.

At some point on the path of courageous grieving, you will notice a subtle but profound internal shift: you start to see reality as it is now. The more you grieve and let go of your version of the idealized reality, the more you can be open to the present. You may suddenly see the vulnerabilities, weakness, and humanness of those who have failed you. Once you have fully grieved and learned to take care of your inner wounds, you will feel much more free; like a heavy weight being lifted off your shoulders, you are no longer trapped by the unexplainable compulsion to alter the past or present reality. You can finally stop searching for the perfection that never existed. As said in the *Tao Te Ching*: 'To hold, you must first open your hand. Let go.'

## Exercise: mourning what might have been

Now, let's make some space to mourn for what you never had. You can do this by recalling a time when you felt sad as a child. Perhaps your parents had upset you, or you were rejected by your peers.

Locate the setting and picture yourself in it. Then, in your journal, start writing. Ideally, write in the present tense as if you were really there again. Describe what you see around you, what you hear, what is happening, what you feel you need and who is around you. Keep writing until you get a sense of your visceral feelings. Feel it in as much detail as possible and feel it with your body and senses.

Then, allow your feeling of sadness to emerge. Breathing more deeply, close your eyes. Now let the memory fill your whole body.

If possible, feel your body as if you were that age, and notice how each of your body parts feels – what is happening to your head, shoulders, back, tummy?

Notice any thoughts that come with the feelings – what might you say if it was entirely safe to do so? If tears come, let them flow; allow your whole body to sob.

If anger comes up in this process, honour that too. Such anger is a healthy, appropriate response to an unjust situation – no child should have to go through such pain and loneliness.

As you remember these experiences, notice how you feel on a visceral level. A cognitive recounting will not suffice, unless it is connected strongly to a bodily feeling, because your memories were stored in your body on a cellular level. The challenge is to find the accurate sense of feeling but not necessarily a storyline.

Truly grieving involves temporarily allowing ourselves to feel very sorry, and sad, even envious or angry. Often, people confuse this with self-pity or as a passive acceptance of defeat. Yet the opposite is true, for nothing is more heroic than facing reality head on. Grieving is not about blaming, but simply an acknowledgement of the tragic nature of events.

It is helpful to think of this as a detoxification process. Sadness is the emotion of release, and grief is appropriate where there has been actual insults and wounding. When you first enter into your grief, you may feel a tremendous weight upon you. It is safe to allow yourself to feel this weight. You do not have to drown in it, nor do you have to dissociate from it. It is by emptying the cup that you can fill it with fresh water.

It is only after you courageously mourn the 'what could have been', you can accept your natural place in this world, and free up the space in your psyche to fully embrace what is in front of you. By welcoming honest sorrow, you can truly let go of your outdated attachments, and invite your natural vitality back in.

## Breaking free from the past

Although not all bad experiences come from your family history, many challenges come with being born into a family that does not understand you. You might have been an exceptionally perceptive child with a family that did not have the capacity to nurture you or to comprehend your gifts. As a sensitive child, you were born with a susceptibility that renders you more vulnerable to feeling hurt. Your siblings, for instance, may have had a similar upbringing but were able to turn a blind eye to the neglect and hurt. Even though most parents do the best they can with what they have and know, many have limited capacities. Even those with the best of intentions may not be able to meet the needs of their naturally intense and sensitive children.

Children who were deprived are left with a lifelong yearning to be seen and heard for who they are. If our emotional needs remain unmet, these longings can become exemplified and misdirected. If we allow the little children inside of us to run the show, we can get on a rollercoaster of unconscious approval-seeking culminating in episodes of disappointment. Some of us continue to be stuck in a co-dependent relationship with those who have hurt or let us down the most, or we become attracted to relationships that are replications of the dysfunctional ones we had growing up. If your family members were once neglectful, the interest they now express in your life can feel phoney. It can be hard to feel close to them, even though you love each other. When you are in touch, dormant anger can erupt from both sides without notice. Or, you may find yourself unconsciously exhibiting 'little boy/girl' behaviours – talking in a particular tone and acting in a certain way. This is because deep down, you still yearn for your family's love and approval.

Perhaps intellectually, you know that your family cannot change the way they are; rationally, you know that the past is in the past. These realizations and acceptances cannot change, however, your current emotional experience – which can still be raw, reactive, volatile, and fuelled by hurt and disappointment. We become stuck because some part of us hopes that through repeating the same things, we might finally experience a different outcome, even though, as adults, we logically know that these patterns will not bring us what we actually want. If we keep ourselves stuck in the position of a child, always wanting the acknowledgement and understanding that we did not get, we end up perpetuating the disappointing loop.

When injustice and wrong have been done, rage and grief are normal responses. However, staying stuck in the sense of betrayal keeps us in the role of the victim. To move forward, we ought to grieve for our past and grow from it. Acceptance does not mean passive surrender. Forgiveness is not for those who have wronged us, but for ourselves. As Martin Luther King Jr famously said, 'Darkness cannot drive out darkness: only light can do that' (1957). We can move forward by acknowledging that everyone did the best they could, given their own predicaments, which might have been fear and ignorance. We come to see and accept that all humans are a combination of contradictions. No one is perfect, and life is not supposed to be. We ought to hold a 'both-and' mentality, leaving some space for the possibility that people can change, while relinquishing the expectation that they will. If you can accept that everything has two sides, you may even come to see the other side of disappointment as freedom: being so traumatically let down and having broken fantasies, you are now free from any illusions, projections and expectations.

In the following guided reflection, we will look at how to break free from reactivity that is fuelled by wounds from the past. We can only truly liberate ourselves by giving up the hope and expectation that those around us will fulfil our deepest wishes. To the best of your ability, see if you can take this opportunity to take matters into your own hands, and take care of yourself as you have never been cared for before.

## Exercise: when you are triggered

1 Think of a time or a situation in your current life or recent past, where you feel that 'the past is in the present'.

You know that some of your current life problems or reactivity are linked to your past when you find yourself reacting to particular circumstances in a way that seems out-of-proportion to the situation. Perhaps you are aware of a surge of pain, anger or hurt that can suddenly well up in certain triggering situations, often with those closest to you. You may feel momentarily 'taken over' by a part of you that seems younger and more primitive.

2 Pause, and take a breath.

Despite differences between what is actually occurring in front of you and the event in your past, do your visceral feelings remind you of an earlier time? Perhaps when you were younger, more vulnerable? Were you misunderstood, humiliated, or bullied for your sensitivity and intensity?

3 Then, ask yourself what intentions, motives or desires are driving your behaviours right now? What is it that you need most from the other person? Here are some words that can be your prompts, all beginning with the letter 'A': attention, approval, appreciation, acknowledgement, applause, adoration or affirmation.

4 Tune in and gently probe the sensation in order to bring up your deeper, cellular memories. When you tune in carefully, you will find that the sense of 'needing', 'wanting' or 'craving' is associated with some physical tension within your body. Once you connect with

those bodily sensations, ask yourself: how old is the person who needs this? Does your yearning belong to a child or an adult?

5 If it belongs to a child, remind yourself that you are a fully functioning, independent adult who can meet these needs yourself or from elsewhere: you are no longer dependent on others. You now have a choice. You can walk away, set boundaries, or say no.

To be truly free, you may want to take this one step further: to embrace, nurse and comfort the lost child inside of you. Loving yourself may not come naturally, especially if you had limited experience of it in your childhood. However, it is within the grasp of all of us to learn to be our own best friend, parent and lover. You can take the hand of the little one inside of you and love him or her with all your heart. You can be that person he or she never had, and tell him or her how much you see, hear and love him or her. You can tell him or her that you recognize how difficult things were, and that you are sorry. Although your old insults and loneliness may have left a scar, you no longer need walk around with an open wound.

In addition, you can seek wisdom and guidance from therapists and spiritual teachers, from cultivating loving adult friendships and partnerships in your current life, and from learning to receive love from others. You can then learn to love yourself.

6 On the other hand, some of your needs may come from your adult self. These needs are usually less emotionally charged. They are rooted in your legitimate rights to reasonable conversation, mutual understanding, basic respect and freedom of speech. Your task here is to acknowledge these needs and take matters into your own hands. With the strength of a self-assured adult, you now have the power to change the way you react to and interact with others. You may put in a request to your family for adequate respect and boundaries in a skilful way. You can become grounded in reality as a self-sustained adult, divorced from a negative communication cycle, and begin an adult-to-adult conversation.

If you continue to interact with your family members with the psyche of a wounded child, you will inadvertently engineer situations that lead to your being treated as one. In contrast, if you can interrupt longstanding and dysfunctional cycles of communication, your family system is bound to change. For example, when you start being assertive about what you can and cannot give, others will have to find a way to renegotiate boundaries with you, and learn to respect your basic rights. Unfortunately, while you have the right to ask for the respect due to you as an adult, others also have the right to continue being who they are. They may or may not react in the way you wish for, but at least you will know that you have done your part – and that is all you can do.

As with most things in life, you have no control over other people. However, you must acknowledge that, unlike that child in the school playground, you are no longer helpless or unsafe. Moving forward, you can affirm your current state with new, positive beliefs about yourself.

7   Finally, you may wish to come up with a new belief about yourself in your own words. When you feel triggered by current incidents or feel engulfed by reactivity, you may use the following statements to remind yourself of your current power:

* *I fully love and accept myself.*
* *Although I had felt powerless and helpless in the past, I can stand up for myself now.*
* *I can walk away from situations that are unfair, abusive or bullying.*
* *I am strong and courageous today.*
* *I am free to express myself.*
* *I appreciate my strengths.*
* *I can feel my power.*
* *I am free to choose in any situation.*
* *I am at peace with myself.*

The past cannot be changed, but we possess the power to shift our inner reality, not just intellectually but on an emotional level. We are not here to harbour self-pity or blame. Instead, we can look to what we can accomplish today to release the toxic emotions we have carried for too long.

# Dealing with difficult family times

Times spent with those who have hurt us in the past, or those who remind us of old wounds, are often the worst triggers for intense negative emotions. If your old wounds were inflicted in your family home, if you are estranged from or have a difficult relationship with your family, spending time with them can be challenging for you now.

There is one inconvenient, unspoken truth in our culture. Given the idealized images portrayed in the media, and reinforced by our culture, around 'family' times such as Christmas, anything less than merry has become taboo. It may be almost impossible to explain to others your complicated family dynamics, or why being at home is actually the most challenging time of the year for you. The fact that there is little acknowledgement and understanding of this issue can further deepen your emotional isolation. However, despite the enforced facade of union and family joy, you are not alone.

In this section we will look at some psychological strategies and mindset changes that may be helpful when we are faced with the real challenge of having to spend time with those who trigger us.

## STRATEGY 1: FORGIVING YOURSELF

Firstly, forgive yourself for being emotionally triggered in the first place. Sometimes we wonder why we are triggered so strongly even when our family members are old, frail, live far away from us and can no longer influence our lives. Even when we have successfully walked away and built a life outside of the family home, when in contact, we can immediately revert to feeling powerless and frustrated as if we were five years old again, or we may start behaving like a raging, uncontrollable teenager. Even when we are living in independent adult bodies, we can feel caged by this strong emotional turmoil. However, there is no need to blame yourself for being triggered, or for having negative feelings in the first place.

Perhaps it would be useful to acknowledge that you will always carry with you a version of your younger self. It may seem that this part of you keeps going back to the same communication cycle, and 'hitting the same wall' with the same people. Although the cycle of repeated disappointment is frustrating, this is actually an indication of your psyche's desire to heal and to move towards integration. It sounds counter-intuitive, but you feel compelled to repeat the same dynamic because part of you still hopes for a different outcome. Your compulsion to keep trying is an unconscious attempt to return to your past in order to clear up old blockages. Thus, thank yourself for having this desire to move towards closure and, whilst it does not lead to the desired outcome, your attempt is itself a sign of resilience, rather than weakness.

## STRATEGY 2: RADICAL ALLOWING

Allowing is not about rushing into forgiveness or false serenity. However, it may be helpful to, at least for the period of time you need to be in direct contact with them, set an intention to 'allow' whatever needs to happen, to happen. You may not like, approve, or accept the way they behave, but you can make a space to 'allow' whatever needs to happen, to happen. What this means is a shift in the way you approach reality – rather than fighting it, you see it for what it is, and you allow those around you to live as they are.

Making judgements and having feelings about the way your family behave is not wrong. Allowing does not mean being a doormat, or accepting abuse. However, many of us fall into the trap of expecting others to be different, and we make needing others to behave in a certain way a precondition for our own peace of mind. Once we fixate on how we believe others ought to change, we become co-dependent on the way they think, feel and act. We pay the high price of our own emotional freedom when we allow ourselves to be stranded by others' temperaments and actions.

No matter how unreasonable, unkind or destructive the behaviour of others seems to you, their actions are always a reflection of *their* truth, and as a fellow human being, you have no choice but to let others live their honest truth. No matter how dysfunctional, the way your family members behave has to do with their own upbringing and their predicaments. Yes, their irrational or offensive behaviours do not make sense. Yes, it is not 'fair' that they fail to understand or appreciate you for who you are, but life is not meant to be fair. The more you fight against the reality of what is, the more you suffer. As the Buddhist perspective suggests, in life, pain is inevitable, but suffering is optional. If your family has been behaving in the same way all these years, what makes you think they can do otherwise?

Remember that true intimacy is only achieved when you can allow the other person to be exactly as they are. The more your mind is preoccupied with how things should be, the more tension you will feel, and the more distance you create between you.

**STRATEGY 3: NOTICING YOUR FIXED PERCEPTION**
Often, our sense of ourselves and of others is rather rigid and restrictive. This is because, as human beings, we have very limited ways of organizing and communicating other than generalizing and categorizing information. However, the reality of life and human dynamics are often more fluid than how we see them. Usually, the moment we come to a fixed view of something, it is already changing. We can observe and learn about this ever-changing quality of life simply by contemplating the force of nature. To borrow a teaching from the Buddha, life is like a river. Despite its outward appearance as one continuous and static thing – 'a river'– that is far from the truth. The river yesterday is not the same as the river today. The river in this moment is not going to be the same as the river in the next moment.

This ever-changing quality applies to people, including you and your family members. As a way of making sense of the messiness of life, we form very fixed views of things: 'He is an angry person', 'I am always going to be upset by this'. Whilst we have these 'impressions' that we and our family members are 'this' or 'that', the reality is that people are constantly in a flow of changing and shifting. If you can see the person in front of you like that flowing river, you will notice that they change each and every moment. Although it is true that some kind of 'personality' or temperament remains, it is an illusion to believe that the person you have seen just now will be exactly the same as the person you will see in a few moments' time. We can even contemplate this from a scientific angle: cell divisions take place in each living being on a continuous basis, and we are constantly in a dual process of decaying and regenerating. Both psychologically and physically, the person in front of you is never the same. He or she is subject to change and the change is continuous, dynamic and fluid.

You may start by noticing the black-and-white, definitive statement that comes up when you judge others as 'this' or 'that'. You can also catch yourself doing this when you use words like 'always' and 'only'. When you notice these fixed ideas (e.g. 'My mother is *always* so insensitive'), you do not have to refute them completely, but you can try to make some room for other possibilities. For instance, consider how *the opposite* of your statement may also be true, even if only on rare occasions. Perhaps your 'selfish' sibling is extremely generous in some other areas of their life, or perhaps there was one time when they behaved entirely differently.

Another way of finding flexibility in your mindset is to change the subject–object relationship around. Do you see yourself as the victim of others' neglect? Who really is depriving you of what you need? You can take radical ownership of your own experience – not in a punitive way, but as a way of introducing more fluidity in your thinking. For instance, if you feel that your parent is not respecting your needs, could it be that YOU are not fully respecting your needs? Are YOU allowing others to violate your boundaries by not saying no and by putting yourself in vulnerable situations? Again, do not fall into blaming yourself – the violation is real and difficult – but focus on what you can do about it yourself.

If you can notice the ever-changing nature of humankind, you may be able to find some solace in knowing that things are not always what they seem and that in each moment there are limitless possibilities for things to be different. Perhaps the biggest challenge here is in holding the paradox of *hope* and *acceptance*. It is wise both to *relinquish any expectation* for things to be different, whilst *allowing some sense of possibility* that things may change any time.

## STRATEGY 4: GETTING BEHIND THE SCREEN

When all things fail, sometimes it is useful to create some mental distance between yourself and the battlefield. One way of doing this is that when you visit your family home, see it as a temporary excursion. You can imagine yourself as an outsider, a 'tourist', or even an anthropologist from Mars.

By adopting the mentality and attitude of that of an anthropologist, you 'get behind the screen' in order to investigate what you see from a scientific and objective perspective. Since you are on an entirely different planet, you have no choice but to suspend your existing ways of understanding the world. Your own logic and assumptions would not apply here, so you can allow yourself to be curious, and at times perplexed, by what you see. You do not expect a simplistic answer to why things are the way they are, or why people do the things they do. After all, you are looking at a species completely different from you. You can even step back and examine their behavioural patterns objectively: do people in this family get caught up in the 'drama triangle' and dance around the roles of victim-rescuer-persecutor? Do certain people get scapegoated? Do people get locked into 'fixed roles' such as the 'black sheep' or 'the golden boy/girl'?

You can play 'make-believe' whilst you are here, you can 'do what the Romans do' when you are in Rome, but deep down you know that the essence of who you are is unaffected by what happens on this excursion. Be an observer, rather than a participant, in order to survive this transient time in your life.

# Exercise: mental rehearsal

We feel anxious when we are not fully prepared for life's challenges. Mental rehearsal is a way to prepare for challenging times. By mentally rehearsing, you can move from being caught in reactivity to being in a prepared, resilient position.

1   Find a time and place where you won't be interrupted. You may wish to recline and close your eyes.

2   Bring to mind your next family visit, the inevitable festive gathering, or any occasion where you will have to be with those who trigger you. Imagine what you will see just before and during the event. Put yourself in the situation and visualize yourself as an active participant, not as a passive observer.

3   Now imagine all the scenarios in which you may be triggered – what might people say to cause you anger? How might the way they look at you create hurtful feelings? Would they give unwarranted comments or advice that drives you into a rage? From the smallest thing to the worst-case scenario, picture what it would be like. You may wish to make some notes in your journal, or make a mental list.

4   Now, develop a contingency plan and then mentally rehearse it.

   a   What can you say to yourself?
   b   What kind of 'mantra' would serve as a good reminder?

5   See if you can summon some of the psychological strategies listed above, or come up with your own.

6   Think about the best way you can handle things, and then mentally imagine yourself doing it.

7   The more options you can come up with in advance, the more adaptive you will be, and the more empowered you will feel.

# 9

# Building emotional resilience

# Moving from defensiveness to openness

One question that often comes up about being an HSP and empath is, 'How do I protect myself?'

Being sensitive means you are naturally more receptive, and in tune with your surroundings; you receive a lot more information – on both the sensory and perceptual level – than those around you. You may feel that as an empath, you tend to absorb others' negative energies and emotions, attract emotional vampires and be overwhelmed by the heaviness of life. You may experience sensory overload, compassion fatigue, and even 'psychic attacks'. Some of the common advice to sensitive people is to visualize an imaginary wall, a 'protective bubble', or cutting cords with those who bring you down. Other practical suggestions include limiting contact with the outside world or avoiding being around certain people and situations. While these strategies can be useful – especially when working with abusive, unhealthy relationship dynamics – they are mostly defensive in nature, and not always sustainable. Many sensitive individuals have yet to find long-term refuge: even when you consciously avoid toxic people, interpersonal events still affect you; even when you limit social interactions, mood swings still seem to happen between four walls.

The biggest problem with a defensive approach is that it reinforces a limited, fear-based sense of self. If you become locked into a fixed view of yourself that is broken, incapable, and must be sheltered and protected, you will have to design your life in a way that is geared towards avoidance rather than growth and expansion. As a result, you may become increasingly frantic and compulsive in your attempts to defend yourself. Your world shrinks, and you become isolated. Eventually, you lose sight of your limitless potential and succumb to a smaller version of yourself.

What is proposed in this book is a different approach, one that may seem counter-intuitive at first. Rather than trying to find ways to defend ourselves against the inevitable and unpredictable nature of life, we open up. Instead of shrinking our being into a small bubble, we expand, and we allow our being to become stronger and bigger so that we can accommodate it all – from aggravation to deep joy and love, so we get to enjoy the full spectrum of human experience.

## TRUE EMPATHY AND EMOTIONAL RESILIENCE

At the core of you is someone who is deeply appreciative of the beauty in life and in the world, and is intensely passionate. But to be with others safely and wholeheartedly as a sensitive person, you must learn to differentiate unregulated emotional contagion from true empathy. Emotional contagion is the phenomenon in which we catch and feel other people's feelings, and it is usually an unconscious process that happens automatically. If you experience too many unregulated emotional contagions, you will constantly be overwhelmed by what you have 'sponged up' from others. Unlike uncontrolled emotional contagions, empathy is a skill. To have the kind of empathic skills that would actually benefit yourself and others means more than just the ability to feel what they feel. It requires psychological maturity and is a skill that can be practised.

World-renowned Stanford University psychologist Carol Dweck (2008) discovered the power of mindset on our human potential. She found that people can either adopt a 'fixed mindset' or a 'growth mindset' – these can have tremendous and pervasive impacts on a person's level of success in life.

Individuals with a 'fixed mindset' assume that their fundamental character and abilities are static and cannot be changed. People with a 'growth mindset', on the other hand, believe that skills and qualities can be attained through effort and deliberate practice. With a fixed mindset, you let each and every challenge and perceived failure define you. With a growth mindset, you know that setbacks are temporary and that life is a process, not an outcome at a fixed point in time. You will go about life with the attitude that everything happens to offer you an opportunity to learn, and that no effort is wasted.

If you apply the 'fixed mindset' to the way you approach your sensitivity, you may surrender to the belief that you are simply 'too sensitive for the world', and avoid any occasions where you might be judged, labelled or harmed, leading to a life where your entire purpose is to avoid being 'found out'. In contrast, with a 'growth mindset', you will come to honour your natural aptitude and qualities, harness your strengths and manage your limitations, and take a proactive stance to cultivate strength and adaptability.

As an emotionally intense person, since you cannot dampen your emotions, it will soon become apparent to you that there is no way 'out' of them, and that the only way is through. In fact, this is the very key to embracing your emotional sensitivity. You become resilient first by embracing painful emotions that arise from within you. Eventually, you can apply the same strategy to external events, stressors, people, and the wider world. No matter how much you try to protect yourself, inevitably the world is busy and imperfect. People are not always nice, and life events are not always fair. Pain and difficulties in life are not the problem, but if you react to them with avoidance, self-condemnation and self-criticism, you may just lose yourself in trying to defend against the ebbs and flows of life. To apply the 'growth mindset' is to harness your strengths as an emotionally intense person. You can choose to thrive on each emotional challenge and see them as a heartening springboard for growth.

Cultivating emotional resilience is like training a muscle. For a long time, it was believed that as we aged, the connections in the brain became fixed. In recent years, the concept of a changing brain has replaced the formerly held belief that the adult brain was pretty much a physiologically static organ or hard-wired after critical developmental periods in childhood. Neuroplasticity, or brain plasticity, refers to the brain's ability to CHANGE throughout life. The human brain has the amazing ability to reorganize itself by forming new connections between brain cells, and research has shown that, in fact, the brain never stops changing through learning.

Becoming a healthy, integrated emotionally intense individual means learning to maintain a core sense of identity without it being swept away by the moment-to-moment changes in your feelings. Your goal is not to have complete control over your emotions. On the flip side, it is not desirable to completely dissociate from them to the point where you feel empty on the inside. Instead, you learn to handle a wide array of feelings, yet not be completely ruled by them.

To have true empathy, you have to be in a place where you are not only able to feel unpleasant feelings but also to tolerate them, and have the confidence that you can survive them. Since what we pick up from others is not always pleasant, true empathy calls for courage and compassion. Even if you do not approve of what you see in other people, you can at least ground yourself to stay conscious of what is happening, without needing to shut down your sensitivity. With enough practice, you will be able to create a heart-space that can accommodate both your tenderness and the pain of the others. Rather than resisting or hardening, you can bring a soft compassion into your awareness; instead of pushing feelings and people away, you hold them. Little by little, it is not that your experience that changes, but your experience of the experience. Your resilience will allow you to feel more alive, rather than limiting yourself to your comfort safety zone. If you can train yourself to nurture your sensitivity and compassion in the most difficult times, you will gradually find a renewed sense of self as an emotionally gifted person. You will feel robust and loving, rather than vulnerable and victimized. Eventually, you will come to see your ability to feel others' emotions not as a bad thing, but as a doorway that connects you to the rest of humanity.

## Exercise: what is the story that you tell yourself?

The stories that we tell ourselves hugely defines how we think and feel, about ourselves and the world. The way we shape our perception is highly selective; if we buy into one narrative of ourselves, e.g. 'I must not outshine others or I will be attacked', that immediately serves as a filter for our perception, and when new information comes in that doesn't fit into this existing framework, we subconsciously bypass it. At the same time, we may selectively reinforce events that fit our existing perception ('The post didn't arrive on time – I knew I couldn't trust anyone in this world!'). Recent findings in neuroscience have validated that our mind does do this. It is called 'schema reinforcement'. In the end, we become more and more stuck in certain patterns, or stories we tell ourselves about who we are and how we ought to behave.

Get a pile of sticky notes, and set a timer for 10 minutes.

Write down words, phrases and memories in response to what emerges when you think of the following:

✳ 'Being sensitive'
✳ 'Feeling things'
✳ 'Passion'
✳ 'Empathy'

Review what you have written, then, ask yourself the following questions:

1 What are some of the messages that you have picked up as you were growing up, or as an adult?
2 What are some of the messages from society or from your surroundings that you might have internalized?

For example:

✳ People who show feelings are weak.
✳ Men should not show vulnerability.
✳ There are positive and negative emotions.
✳ 'Sensitive' people are weak.
3 Have you somehow bought into the belief that you are 'too much for the world'?
4 What are some of the defensive strategies that you have used to protect yourself against the world? How are they working for you?
5 What do you do when you feel negative emotions – do you become immersed in them, or do you avoid them?
6 Do you see emotions as threats?
7 Do you believe that your brain is fixed, or do you trust that emotional resilience can be cultivated?

# Having a secure base

It is impossible to stay open to the world when you do not feel safe in it. As human beings, when we don't feel safe, our natural tendency is to freeze, contract, fight or run away. Thus, the first step of openness practice is to cultivate an internal sense of safety.

Because of your sensitivity, you not only react to life's events more intensely, but you tend to remain emotionally impacted for a longer period of time. You may have a hard time returning to your emotional 'baseline' after a crisis. If you find that you tend to go on an emotional downward spiral and end up in a state of despair, this may be because, deep down, you do not feel safe in the world. Even though logically, you know that you are physically safe, you may still feel psychologically vulnerable on the inside. Sometimes, you don't feel like a strong adult, but a child that needs holding and protecting. When negative events happen, you do not have the faith that when you fall, there is something there to hold you. This sense of despair is linked to not having what psychologists call a 'secure base' within yourself.

Psychological studies have found that children who have good attachment to their caregivers can trust and use them as a 'secure base', which also serves as a springboard for them to safely explore the world. In a series of psychological experiments known as the 'strange situation', children were put into a room with toys lying around while their caregiver came in and out. Researchers observed the children's reactions in order to determine their attachment patterns and how they coped with separation anxiety. They found that children who had a good attachment relationship with their parents reacted drastically differently from those without. Although the securely attached children showed signs of distress when their parents left the room, as soon as their parents returned, they were able to instantly self-regulate, and bonded with others again. They felt safe enough to explore and play in their parents' quiet presence. In contrast, children without a sense of having a 'secure base' demonstrated greater and longer distress when their parents left; even when left in a room full of toys, they were too frightened to play. Many of them remained distressed and mistrustful even as their parents returned (Ainsworth *et al.*, 2015).

The founder of human attachment theories, John Bowlby, stated that all of us, from the cradle to the grave, are happiest when life is organized as a series of excursions, long or short, from the secure base (2005). Without the knowledge that we have something solid to come back to, however, it is very difficult to be courageous. From a young age, we rely on having a 'secure base' to give us emotional freedom and courage. When we have a secure base, life becomes a fun adventure, a roller coaster ride. We can enjoy the journey knowing that we are fundamentally safe and have a 'home' to go back to. Without a secure base, bad events may leave us disconcerted, and feeling that all signs of threats are nightmares that will never end. As children, our caregivers provide us with a secure base. As adults, however, we have to find it within ourselves. This may be particularly difficult for those of us who did not have the experience of a secure base when we were little.

To develop a secure base as an adult means to learn to take care of yourself, to befriend emotions that arise in you, and to gradually develop the confidence that you can bounce back from whatever life throws at you. In her book *Feel the Fear and Do It Anyway*, Susan Jeffers (2012) states that fear is the belief that you would not be able to handle what might happen if you took action, and that the way to rise above fear is to believe in your ability to handle whatever it is that you face in life. Similarly, in his book *Daring to Trust*, David Richo (2011) suggests that the foundation of adult trust, love and intimacy is not the Pollyanna belief that 'you will never hurt me', but 'I trust myself with whatever you do'.

With a secure base within yourself, you do not have to fight, judge, deny or rationalize your emotions. You can count on your inner strength so that you no longer feel at the mercy of drastic mood swings. Once you have developed a sense of internal trust, even when faced with tremendous uncertainties, you know on some level that you will not emerge from situations feeling completely groundless. You will no longer need to rely on others for reassurance or safety because you know that you have yourself to come back to. Eventually, your confidence in your own ability to come back from emotional storms can act as your 'home base', the part of your life that remains unperturbed no matter what.

The following exercises set the foundation for your secure base. The short meditation will help you to remember how safety feels. We will then identify things in your life that nourish and support you, and compose your physical and psychological secure base.

# Exercise: safe place meditation

The following visualization exercise can help you to find a sense of safety within yourself. The goal is for you to feel safe within yourself not only intellectually, but also emotionally and physically. For years, counsellors and therapists have used the 'safe place visualization' as a way of helping people heal from even the most severe forms of trauma. This is an effective exercise that has helped many individuals who initially struggle to find some stability within themselves.

1  Find a relatively quiet place, and relax.
2  Start by imagining a place where you feel safe. If the word 'safety' feels too loaded or difficult to find, do not stress too much about it – you are not alone. You can simply imagine a place where you feel relatively 'good', or calmer than usual. It does not have to be perfect. It does not have to be a physical place either – it may be a place from memory, somewhere you have travelled to in the past, or from a dream; alternatively, you can simply create something abstract and symbolic in your mind.
3  Now picture the details of your peaceful place. Are you sitting, standing or perhaps lying down? Maybe you are walking around, or doing any one of a variety of activities. Perhaps you are alone or maybe you are with company. You may have a pet or an animal by your side. When you look around you, what else do you see? Notice what comes into your eyes, including the colours, various shapes, objects, plants, etc.
4  Then focus on the sounds you may hear, including silence. Notice the sounds both far away and close to you, the louder ones and the subtle ones.
5  Now think about any smells you may notice in this place.
6  Also notice the pleasant physical sensations in your body whilst you enjoy this safe place. Notice any skin sensations: the earth beneath you or whatever is supporting you in that place, the temperature, any movement of air, and anything else you can touch.
7  Allow yourself to fully immerse in the sights, sounds and sensations around you. You can choose to linger there a while, just enjoying the peace and serenity.
8  Now whilst you're in your peaceful and safe place, you might choose to give it a name; this may be one word or a phrase that you can use to bring back the image at any time.
9  You can leave whenever you want to, just by opening your eyes and being aware of your surroundings. See if you can maintain the feeling of calm from your peaceful place as you return to your everyday life.

## Exercise: building your altar

If you find the idea of an imaginary safe place too difficult or elusive, you can start by identifying some of the more external, tangible things that support you in your present environment.

The construction of your personal, psychological and physical secure base can be likened to the process of building a personal altar. In many psycho-spiritual traditions, a personal altar refers to a sacred space dedicated to elements that are important and supportive to you. It is a supportive space where you find both serenity and inspiration.

Take out your journal, and ask yourself the following questions:

1 In the past, when you have been disturbed or thrown off balance, what was helpful/what brought you back to 'balance'?
2 Do you have any morning or evening rituals or routines that give you a sense of stability?
3 What are some of the things you do that are guaranteed to give you pleasure?
4 What are the things that remain unchanged within you no matter what (e.g. your values)?
5 What is it that you have control over?
6 What gives you joy?
7 What are the relationships that you feel loved in, nourished by – in a real sense?
8 From whom and from what do you gain appreciation?

Make a list of what gives you a sense of stability. These can be things that give you pleasure, a feeling of love, or balance. They can range from the small to the significant, the mundane to the divine. For instance, it may include the morning coffee that gives you immense pleasure, but also your relationship with God or your spiritual source. It is best if it comes from a variety of sources, as you are bound to feel fearful if you only rely on one source, like your romantic partner.

Write these things on a piece of paper and put it somewhere visible to remind yourself that no matter what happens in the outside world, these things are your constant foundation.

# Befriending your emotions

Emotionally sensitive individuals are more affected by life's ups and downs. Due to the depth of your emotions, you can access a more expansive reality, and experience strong attachments to places, people and situations. The flux of life – people leaving, eras ending, relationships ending – may hurt more for you. As Elaine Aron, author of *The Highly Sensitive Person* suggests, 'Being easily aroused and having strong emotional reactions are two facts of the sensitive person's life' (Aron, 1996). This quality is at the core of your nature, and although it is painful at times, your ability to see and feel so much also serves as the root of your integrity and moral sensitivity. You may struggle to do what others do – denying, brushing off or dampening strong feelings. When a worry sows its seed in your mind, you may struggle to get rid of it; you find yourself dwelling in thoughts until the problem is solved. Your friends and family may advise you to 'not think too much', to 'sleep on it', or to 'go get a drink' and distract yourself. These temporary strategies may work for them, but you continue to struggle to settle with peace. This is the result of a neurological difference, rather than some kind of defect. Yet to others, you may appear neurotic or even obsessive. Sadly, nowadays we live in an emotion-phobic culture that encourages the silencing of feelings, especially the perceived 'negative' ones.

Sometimes, your sensitivity brings you strong waves of emotions that your cognitive mind is not ready for. More often than not, those emotions are trying to tell you something, and are there to serve you, even if they don't feel friendly at that moment. Emotions, spelt 'e-motion', also means energy in motion. Each emotion has its own energetic qualities, and serves a distinctive function. The absence of emotions does not bring peace, but depression. The opposite of happiness is not unhappiness, but apathy. In fact, the definition of clinical depression is when things become colourless, devoid of energy. In other words, emotions are the source of our vitality, signposts to a fulfilling life. Therefore, instead of trying to get rid of emotions, we are going to look at how we can embrace, befriend, manage and harness them.

Authentic feelings arise naturally, and you have little control over what comes and knocks on your door. If you do not have the confidence that you can deal with emotional intensity, you will feel like you are constantly on guard, in fight-or-flight mode, and unsettled in your own presence.

If you have felt like the victim of your own emotional storms, the idea of befriending your emotions may seem like an unachievable goal. Without having found safety and stability within yourself, constantly being carried away with the emotional ups and downs can leave you feeling nothing but powerless.

Not only do we need a physical and psychological 'secure base', we also need an emotional secure base. In order to find that place of refuge and inner peace, we need to find a deep-seated sense of spacious stillness that is undisturbed by the emotional ups and downs that go on on the surface. This is not to be confused with the suppression of feelings, apathy or detachment. In fact, it does quite the opposite – finding this refuge space within yourself gives you the stability and strength that deepens your presence, patience and connection with the world around you. It is what allows your heart to stay open, rather than close down.

The idea of opening to your emotions is not new. For centuries, spiritual practitioners of various traditions have been working towards this through mindfulness practice. Mindfulness has become a buzzword in our world today; whilst it has only recently been embraced by Western psychology, it is an ancient practice found in a number of Eastern philosophies, including Buddhism, Taoism and Yoga. It is indeed a powerful practice, and evidence has mounted up to support it as an effective way to reduce stress, increase joy and self-awareness, enhance emotional intelligence, and undo various unhelpful emotional, cognitive and behavioural patterns.

Mindfulness can be defined in a variety of ways, but they all basically come down to: paying attention to the present moment with an intention to cultivate curiosity and compassion. Despite the usual misconception, mindfulness can be practised inside or outside of formal meditation. It can take a number of different forms, from 'formal' practices such as sitting/breathing exercises, to other practices aimed at cultivating a continuity of awareness in your daily living.

There seems to be a misconception that people you see sitting on a mat have all reached a state of serenity, and that idea may be so far from your own experience that it has made you decide 'I cannot meditate', or 'I am bad at meditating'. Yet if you ask anyone who practises mindfulness regularly, you will know that complete serenity is a far cry from what actually happens. The mind, especially for the emotionally intense, is constantly busy, with thinking, planning, reminiscing and judging... this is completely natural. Mindfulness is not about getting rid of all thoughts and feelings, but to create a space for them in which to come and go, so that we no longer feel trapped in them. The intention here is to practise getting behind your emotions, rather than dwelling on them.

With sufficient and consistent practice you will have cultivated a sense of resilience, to approach emotions arising within yourself with a kinder and softer open heart. Then, you will be ready to break down the barrier between you and the world that has kept you separate and painfully alone.

## Excercise: befriending your emotions

In contrary to the urban myth, mindfulness practice is not something that you have to do by sitting on an uncomfortable cushion for hours, chanting 'omm'. In fact, you can try to have an experience of it right here, right now.

1  Bring up an unpleasant feeling – name it in the way you usually would (it may be 'fear','anger' or 'shame').
2  Anchor your mind with breathing. Pay attention to your desire to run away from the unpleasantness of your experience. You may also notice your mind chattering away; it may be judging what you are feeling, or trying to give it explanations, or trying to reason it away. It is natural that it does that: see if you can gently bring your mind back, without condemning yourself for being distracted in the first place.

3  Notice any cognitive thoughts that come with your feelings, for example 'I am irritated'. Then, see if you can refrain from fuelling your feelings further with thoughts.

4  Turn your thought from a personal one into a neutral description. For instance: from 'I am irritated' to 'This is irritation'.

5  Even though it feels unpleasant, trust that your feeling is not hostile. When we first start quieting our minds and attending to what arises, it is not unusual for us to deem our feelings and thoughts 'bad' and wanting to abruptly stop them. We may even start blaming ourselves for having these thoughts.

6  Consider this: you have these thoughts because you had needed them to live in this world. Part of you believes that it needs to be on guard and must hold onto these ideas for you to function effectively in this world. That part of you is trying to be helpful. Although it doesn't feel helpful, and logically is not helpful, trust for now that it was there for a friendly reason. See if you can acknowledge that, and gently say 'thank you' to it.

7  Continue to do this for a few more minutes. Your feelings may be pleasant, unpleasant or neutral. We have a tendency to want to move away from the unpleasant. See if you can stay with it – perhaps you can say to yourself, 'For just one more second, just one more second, and one more...' and bring your awareness back to your breathing. If distracting or self-condemning thoughts come back, gently put them aside.

8  After a few more minutes, you may pause, and congratulate yourself for having taken this time to cultivate kindness and openness towards yourself. You have now begun the process of cultivating emotional resilience.

9  Starting from today, set an intention to expand, inch by inch, a little every day, your tolerance for your own negative emotions and the unpleasant events around you. Remind yourself that all your fear and anxiety come from negative experiences in the past. However, no matter what happened then, you are safe now, and can handle a lot more than you think. You have a choice to stay connected to your secure base, to attend to the good in your life, and to feel gratitude rather than fear. You may bring this practice into your day-to-day life by setting the intention each morning: 'Today, I aspire to stay open to all that is to see, to all that is to hear, to feel, and to know, with a sense of kindness and openness'.

You can also become more mindful of the times in your daily life when you feel an urge to avoid, to numb out and to close down.

# Listening to your feelings

The traditional Western medical model tends to look at health from an absolute, reductionist perspective that rarely takes into account an individual's whole-body wellness. Conventional medicine is sometimes called allopathic medicine. Allopathy – derived from the Greek word *allo* meaning 'other' – is based on the theory that treatment of a disease means suppressing any symptoms. In this model, symptoms are seen as malicious intrusions that must be countered with drugs. As you probably have experienced, however, suppressing your symptoms often leads to nothing more than your body creating other symptoms in protest. Such an approach does not address the core issue within but instead leads us to lose trust in the wisdom of our bodies and minds.

A disease-oriented approach fosters fear-based thinking. Many of us have adopted this mentality through cultural conditioning. As a result, when we experience any pain or symptoms, we naturally begin to think that we have done something wrong or that there is something fundamentally wrong with us.

Leaving the allopathic model behind, we find that the human body possesses an innate ability to heal itself and to strive for – and reach – homeostasis. This view is not a new one: it predates allopathy and has, for many centuries, been the core philosophy of many healing cultures. Only recently has modern science begun to validate the notion that our bodies are intrinsically self-healing, self-regulating and self-correcting. For proof that we, as humans, are infinitely adaptive, look only at the biological reality within our cells. Every second, our cells are endlessly working to bring us back to a natural state of equilibrium. Each cell is a living, dynamic unit that continuously adjusts and adapts to its environment, seeking balance. In the body's quest for wholeness, our cells not only heal themselves but also regenerate and replace cells that have been damaged.

Looking at our health in this way, we can see that many of the 'unpleasant' things we experience are nothing more than our body's built-in mechanisms to help us deal with external stressors. When you feel nauseated, it is because your body is trying to heal itself by expelling toxins. The unpleasant symptoms of nausea and vomiting reflect your body's best efforts to adapt to its new stressor and to fight infection. Your sickness, then, does not imply that something is wrong with you, but that your system is functioning and working its way back into wellness.

Now, consider: what if your psyche operates in the same way? What if, like your body, your mind is perfect in its design?

All your emotions contain information that is indispensable to your survival. In fact, neurological research has shown that when people cannot access their emotions due to illness or trauma, they also become unable to make decisions, make social interactions, or live a meaningful life (Damasio, 2006). Perhaps pain and loss are not just a part of being human but are also essential ingredients of all growth, transformation and regeneration. Being able to flip around how you view your difficulties is a big part of such growth.

However challenging they may seem, your emotions are your allies. Your anger is there to teach you about assertiveness and boundary setting. Sadness is your doorway to compassion and connections, grief helps you let go of what needs to be released so you can make room for the new, anxiety tells you what matters to you and envy turns you towards what you reject within yourself.

In fact, even your 'problematic behaviours' are often pointing to something in your intense nature that needs to be honoured. Your 'addiction' to pleasures such as eating is a container for your extraordinary sensual excitabilities and a reflection of how much joy and pleasure you get from life. Your 'workaholism' is an indicator of your drive. Your chronic anxiety comes from your existential desire to actualize your full potential and an expression of your love for life. All symptoms are, in some way, an invitation for you to fully express yourself. If you could recognize them as such, you could start channelling the misdirected energies towards growth and expansion.

Like your body, your mind is an intelligent, self-correcting mechanism that is always striving towards wholeness and growth. Your psychological system is infinitely adaptive, and through its creativity, it has devised strategies to alert you to your growth and help you survive.

Therefore, even during your bleakest hours, try to challenge your own fixed, narrow perception that what you are experiencing is 'bad'. Instead of judging and resisting, see if you can take a moment to contemplate the possible messages within your difficulties – they may well be serving a bigger purpose that you do not yet see.

The old paradigm is linear and says that symptoms are 'bad' and need to be eradicated; the new paradigm says that problems are signals from our deepest self that it is time to change. Certain ways of being might have been useful and functional until this point, but have now become obsolete or detrimental. You have an inherent wisdom that strives towards wholeness and growth. Your emotional intensities will not stop, but by realizing that these emotional crises are a natural part of your growth and not somehow symptoms of a 'sickness', you can feel more grounded while navigating the ups and downs of life. When you realize your capacity for healing and thriving, peace will emerge, powerful enough to change the course of your life and your mission. As the Reverend Martin Luther King, Jr once said: 'Human salvation lies in the hands of the creatively maladjusted' (1995).

# Exercise: listening to your emotions

Every emotion has a function, even the so-called negative ones. They play a significant role in our lives by motivating us, preparing us for the necessary behaviours, and signalling us to our needs and wants.

Reflect on the following:

1 Think of some examples when your emotions have prompted you to take the necessary action? (For example, feeling anxious about a decision may be a sign that you have not sufficiently prepared yourself, or that you need more information to proceed. Your anxiety can prompt you to take action: asking for help, gathering more data, revising your options, etc.)

2 When was the last time an emotion helped you to overcome an obstacle or propelled you to make the necessary changes? (For example, feeling annoyed at work so that you had to speak up for yourself.)

During the coming week, when you notice an emotion arising, consider the possible messages embedded in them. Here are some hints and prompts, but the list is by no means inexhaustible and should never override your instinct:

Anger
✳ Has someone violated my rights, or overstepped my limits?
✳ What are some of my needs that have been denied or compromised?
✳ What boundaries must be asserted or restored?
✳ Should I adjust some of my social and interpersonal rules?

Anxiety
✳ Do I have enough clarity about what is within my control and what is not?
✳ For what is within my control, have I prepared sufficiently?
✳ Do I have enough information about the situation? What further actions can I take?
✳ If it is beyond my control, can I release my attachment to a fixed outcome?
✳ What am I ultimately most fearful of?

## Fear and panic

* Have I been confusing an old fear with the actual threat in front of me?
* Was there psychological trauma that has been frozen in time and needs to be addressed?
* What can I do to protect myself now, as a mature adult?

## Sadness

* What needs to be mourned and released?
* Am I holding onto a fantasy, and refusing to let go of 'what might have been'?
* How can I live more fully in the present and embrace what is in front of me?
* Have I been feeling lonely, and do I need to connect with others?

## Frustration

* What are some of my expectations that have not been met?
* Have I been repeating the same behavioural or relationship cycle?
* Can I change the way I communicate my needs or change my expectations?
* What resources or support might I need to change my course?

## Numbness and boredom

* Am I under-stimulated in some aspects of my life?
* Have I been avoiding thinking about certain issues, or feeling certain feelings?
* Have I been using detachment and apathy as a defence?
* What must be made more conscious in my life now?
* What can I do to restore vitality?

## Joy

* Is this a hedonistic pleasure or does it lead to sustainable happiness? (It can be both.)
* What more can I do to increase hope, delight and invigoration in my life?
* Is my joy pointing to my calling?
* What does my joy tell me about my values?
* Do I get too attached to pleasure and get anxious about it ending?
* How can I make sure I preserve the time and space for playfulness and creativity in my life?

# Riding the waves of change

One of the major things that stops us from staying open to ourselves and others is harsh self-judgement. When a disappointment or a crisis first happens, we inevitably feel pain, disappointment, fear, etc. Yet we often add another layer of suffering by fighting against these feelings – judging them, condemning them, denying them, believing that we 'should not' have them. Rather than being compassionate with ourselves, as we would with a dear friend, we become our own worst enemy.

Many emotionally intense people have a negative view of themselves, and a tendency to have a default belief that they have done something wrong or that there is something wrong with them. When bad events happen, and as the feelings of hurt or anger arise in you, you may hear your internal critic saying 'Why am I so sensitive?', 'I shouldn't make a big fuss', or other 'I should not' phrases. These negative thoughts originally came from society's oppressive view of those in the minority, or from the judgement of those around you, yet somehow they have been internalized by you.

Perhaps because the groundlessness of having so little control in life frightens us, our small, fearful selves have to come up with these mental chatters to assert some sense of control. Part of us believes that if we criticize ourselves enough, we can stop bad things from happening. Although it is painful and inaccurate, that part of us would rather believe that it is 'our fault' that bad things happen – at least this feels like a more familiar narrative – rather than having to face the dauntingly unpredictable nature of life and our powerlessness in the face of it. Unfortunately, our old 'comfort zone' is not comfortable; our attempt to control and find refuge in mental explanations and self-condemnation is exactly what keeps us stuck and closed down.

The reality is that if we allow them to surface and process them, most emotions last only a few minutes. What scientists have found is that the reason we experience extended periods of depressed mood or anxiety is that we continue to fuel these emotional energies with our internal dialogue, internal tension and preconception about how we ought to feel, and what not to feel. What we fight, persists. In essence, what we are doing is reviving the initial emotion again and again with mental chatters that sound like a broken record.

The renowned spiritual teacher Pema Chodron (2009) encourages us to 'let go of our storyline, but stay with the energy'. If you can separate your thoughts and judgement from the pure, visceral aspect of your experience, you will see that these strong feelings are nothing but energy that needs to go through you. Although the goal is not to make your feelings go away, if you can hang in there, you may find that the nature of emotions means they will change, and shift, in one way or another.

Building emotional resilience is to practise observing our initial reactions with an unbiased attitude, without adding another layer of judgement, fear and rejection on top. Pain and disappointment in life are inevitable, and our goal is not to escalate them. Instead, you can find some ground under your feet by recognizing that change is the only constant in life, and beginning to see all experiences, good or bad, as nothing more than the building blocks of your human experience.

Simply by contemplating nature, we come to see that things, including unpleasant feelings, come and go, and our perceptions are not as solid and fixed as they seem. We can find the resemblance of the changeable nature of our emotions in nature. As a season comes, it is already going. As a leaf starts to flourish, it is simultaneously on its way to decay. Within the confines of language, when we speak of 'autumn' and 'winter', we think of them as definitive concepts, when actually, it is not possible to pinpoint the one moment when 'autumn 'turns into 'winter'. The same can be said about our thinking and feelings. As a thought arises, it is already on its way to leaving, unless you fuel it again with negativity and compulsion. When a bad day, a bad patch, a bad experience comes, it is already on its way out.

One of the ways in which we can apply this wisdom in our dealings with intense emotions is to focus on our raw, sensory experience. We can simply attend to what philosophers call primary (size, shape, mass) and secondary (colour, sound, odour, taste) qualities of what is going on. As the elements compound into forms, they are at the same time decomposing and disintegrating. You may stare at your feelings for long enough until they lose their form and structure, dissolve and eventually leave your system. So as best you can, don't hold onto any of your feelings or perceptions too tightly, and rest assured in the fact that, however unpleasant, all things pass.

## Excercise: finding refuge in sensory experience

1  Find a time and space for this exercise. Whether you are sitting, standing, or lying down, turn your attention inwards and scan your body from top to bottom. Examine whatever physical sensations or emotions you are experiencing – they may be pleasant, unpleasant or neutral. You may struggle to find or feel anything – and that's okay too – simply attend to that feeling of nothingness.

2  Now, consciously bring up a mild unpleasant feeling. It may be a mild irritation, some anxiety, or grief caused by physical pain. If you are new to this practice, it is best to start with something not too challenging.

3  Bring your conscious awareness to any 'storyline' that is fuelling, or perpetuating your unpleasant feeling. The storyline may go like this: 'I am irritated because the woman next to me is talking too loudly'. Or, 'My pain will never stop'. If we give our storyline attention, it will usually fuel itself and generate more thoughts, and even new feelings – of anger, fear, sense of indignation – these feelings may then generate more thoughts, and the cycle continues. Whatever thoughts or beliefs are fuelling your cycle, simply notice them non-judgementally.

4  If you can catch your stream of thoughts, try to separate them with your raw, sensory-based experience. Instead of dwelling in the content of the thoughts and allowing them to perpetuate themselves endlessly, shift your awareness to the energetic and visceral aspect of your feeling. As you bring up this feeling, what kind of sensations

do you find in your body? Is there any one that is calling out for your attention? If more than one sensation arises, pick one and contemplate its texture and qualities.

- ▶ Is it warm or cool?
- ▶ Is it moving or still?
- ▶ Can you give it a colour, a shape, a texture?
- ▶ Can you represent it with a visual image or a symbol?

5  As you attend to the sensation, see if it changes, even just subtly and slowly. It's okay if it doesn't. The goal here is not to 'do' anything with it or to make it go away, but merely to stay with the experience and observe how it works.

6  Continue to observe the transient nature of your experience, for as long as you can, or until your feeling dissolves itself.

7  Finally, set an intention for the next week. See if you can take each arising emotion as an opportunity to strengthen your emotional resilience. Remind yourself that your emotions are not threats, but simply energies – pay attention to the physical sensations that go through you as you feel them, even if they are unpleasant; you may say to yourself, 'There is a very strong sensation going through me right now. I feel heat in my heart and it is almost achy'.

Despite what your mental chatter says ('I am going to die', 'I can't live with this'), remind yourself that these energies are ultimately safe. Allow them to flow through you, so they can leave your system. Even if the sensation is really strong, this is a sign that you are alive. You do not have to like, or approve of your feelings to do this. You can even say 'I don't like this, I don't approve of it, but it is here. I learn to accept it'.

Gradually, you will see that you need not be afraid of the energies that you have previously labelled as 'bad'. They are just energies. Those are just labels. They are not going to last forever, unless you fuel them with an endless stream of internal dialogue.

Eventually, you will learn to 'ride the waves' of life's ups and downs. As Jon Kabat-Zinn (2009) says, 'You can't stop the waves, but you can learn to surf!'.

# Opening to life

Once you have created some internal space around the coming and going of your emotions, you are prepared to open to the events that happen in life, and to the world around you.

Our minds have a tendency to fixate on an idea of how we think things should be. Yet life is full of surprises. Events inevitably end, people die and objects perish. The reality is that not all people are loving and trustworthy, and life is not always fair. No matter how hard we try to control things, we cannot. Despite our strong desire to hold onto certainty, most of our lives unfold in ways that are beyond our control.

It takes practice to learn to flow with life's natural order. Before mastering that skill, our natural reaction to the flux of life is to hold on to what is passing and resist letting go of what is coming to an end. Even if we are not consciously aware of it, most of us try to avoid getting in touch with our fundamental powerlessness. Because having an idea about the future gives us a sense of power, we start coming up with judgements and preferences about how we think things 'should be'. However, if we allow ourselves to fixate on what we believe 'should' or 'should not' happen, we become threatened by life's surprises. We forget that our expectations and preferences are ultimately our mind's fabrication, based on the limited information we have. We lose sight of the fact that our views are only limited, and there are forces beyond our control that operate outside of our sphere of knowledge. In fact, what we think serves us may not ultimately do so, and what we want may not be what we need. When we try to fight life instead of yielding to its natural flow, we get caught up in disappointment and frustration.

The goal of opening to life is not to make the world as you would have it, but to develop the ability to take it as it is. When sharing his secret to happiness, the great philosopher Jiddhu Krishnamurti said, 'Do you want to know what my secret is? I don't mind what happens'. Practising to expand rather than contract means opening up to life's limitless possibilities, and becoming free from your need to hold onto what you think is good and to push away what you think is bad. In the

Buddhist tradition, it is said that we tend to get caught up in the following 'eight worldly winds': praise and blame, success and failure, pleasure and pain, fame and disrepute (Melander, 2012). Resisting the flow of life is only going to perpetuate your limited view of yourself, and this feeds into the limiting belief that you cannot tolerate life because of your sensitive nature. Liberation from fears and worries comes not from the belief that the world will give you what you want since that kind of pleasure-driven relief is only short-lived. Real freedom comes from the conviction that no matter what the outcome is, you will either deal with it or grow from it. Instead of being attached to a particular outcome (e.g. I want that very job, that very partner), you can focus on growing from increased adaptability. With consistent practice, you can feel pleasure without clinging to it or worrying about its ceasing, and you can feel pain without perpetuating it.

While I have been calling it a 'practice', opening to life is more of a mindset, a mentality, a way of approaching life and its challenges, rather than something you 'do'. Rather than a once-and-for-all event, think of it more like an intention, with which you cultivate a friendly attitude and a loving relationship with the world. Instead of expending endless energy in resisting reality, you welcome whatever changes or events arise, you peacefully co-exist with them and allow them to change you. Ultimately, you will feel more and more free by expanding the range of life experiences you welcome into your world.

You will still be extremely sensitive, painfully receptive, and acutely aware of your surroundings, yet rather than experiencing the external world as a threat, you can also see it as a fertile playing field that allows you many opportunities to expand, adapt and become more resilient.

## Excercise: harnessing a moment of openness

1 Bring up a time when there has been a shift in your perspective on a matter that involves hurt or aversion towards yourself or others. It may be a time when someone wronged you and you decided to forgive them, or when you shifted some fixed beliefs about yourself and found

self-compassion. It does not have to be anything major or significant; openness is sometimes nothing more complicated than a shift in the way you think or feel about something. What initially took the appearance of cruelty, failure and insult, may turn out to be a critical learning or precious moment, and we often only realize the bigger picture in retrospect.

2  Examine what has helped you to experience the shift. Its antecedents may be something subtle or profound: you might have been moved by nature, inspired by a beautiful poem, or heard a touching song. Perhaps you had a change of heart by remembering all the positive things about the person in front of you. Or, maybe you were suddenly able to see the vulnerabilities in the ones who have wronged you.

3  Now, bring your awareness to the sensations around your heart area, and see if you can locate a sense of space. Imagine breathing from your heart. If you pay close attention to what is happening within you, you may find that there is a part of you that is feeling warm, vibrant and expansive. This feeling of warmth and passion is at the core of your sensitivity and who you are – the emotional ups and downs are simply passing clouds, and what is underneath remains unperturbed. Tune into closely and absorb fully what it feels like when you can move from a rigid and fixed negative perspective, or from a place of fear and anger, towards a place of love and compassion.

4  Now bring up another event, situation, or a person, that you currently feel negatively towards. Consider the following statements. You may wish say them out loud, or contemplate them in writing:

✱  'Right now, I believe that this is a negative event. But I am open to the possibility that the opposite might also be true.
Even though I am not aware of what the embedded gifts or lessons might be, I am open to the possibility that what is happening may have value.'

✱  'Perhaps my negativity is a sign that I have been holding back from love and empathy. It may be that this person has come into my life to provide me an opportunity to grow, or to heal. Or, this is happening so that I can begin to notice some recurring patterns in my life that I need to change.'

✱  'Life has orchestrated this so that I need to somehow harness a wider perspective, rise above the immediate situation, and create a bigger story beyond the surface.

Even though it is irritating/disappointing/worrying, even though I do not yet know why or how, I choose to believe that there is some value in this experience.'

&#42; 'I intend to open to the many possibilities and perspectives on this matter.'

5   Relax, and allow these thoughts to sink into your subconscious mind. Doing mental exercises like this one is like planting a seed. You can trust that the seed of wisdom will gradually grow, even without your conscious willing or knowing.

6   Finally, congratulate yourself for taking the time to harness psychological adaptability and resilience.

# Trusting life

Practising openness to the ebb and flow of life is easier said than done. Many people have found that building a sense of trust in something greater than themselves acts as a gateway to emotional resilience.

In recent years, mental health clinicians and scholars have begun to validate the power of faith when it comes to our well-being. Empirical studies have found that having some form of trust in something bigger than ourselves helps us to deal with life's stressors such as natural disasters, illnesses, bereavement and separation from loved ones. Trusting is not about worshipping a deity, but about harnessing a sense of trust that our lives are unfolding in a benevolent cosmic order that we cannot perceive. As Steve Jobs (2005) reminded us, 'You can't connect the dots looking forward; you can only connect them looking backwards. So you have to trust that the dots will somehow connect in your future.'

Trusting life is not just a concept, but a continuous practice. You may find it helpful to dig deep within yourselves, to find a source that you can depend on to guide you in this messy, unpredictable world. Some call this source God, others call it the Universe, the Divine Spirit, or simply 'the higher power'. All spiritual practices involve cultivating an attitude of surrendering, letting go, accepting what is, believing that 'everything happens for a reason', yielding to God's plan, karma, or trusting the Divine order. It is important that you find the words that resonate with you. Even when your mind cannot yet perceive it, you can choose to believe that someone, or something, is taking care of it all. When defined in this way, spirituality is not about religion, but about a sense of faith in the natural order of life.

Learning to trust life may require you to heal from the life pattern of being a 'parentified child'. Many emotionally sensitive and gifted individuals have automatically taken on the role of the 'little adult' in their family. Parentification occurs when a child is put in a position where they have to grow up 'too soon', is burdened with a huge amount of responsibility, or is made to be a parent to their parents (see also Chapter 5). Gifted children automatically take on this role because of their natural competence. For many highly empathic children, because they have the warmth, compassion and depth that is beyond normal, their family members have come to lean on them emotionally. Children who are parentified often grow up feeling hyper-vigilant and hyper-responsible. They are used to being the ones who make sure that everything is in order, and to being responsible for meeting not just their own needs but also those of others. They are programmed into feeling that if they let go of the control wheel for just a minute, things will go wrong.

When bad things happen, letting go and opening yourself to the limitless possibilities life has to offer is often the hardest, yet the most needed lesson for the emotionally intense and sensitive person. Many of us have a hard time relinquishing control, because of a deep-rooted belief that we must work hard to earn what we need, and to fight in a world of scarcity. In many ways, we are programmed to believe that life cannot be easy. Therefore, it takes conscious and consistent practice to rewire our minds; it takes humility and patience, and is achieved through a consistent practise of letting go of our own fixed views. This is often easier to do in 'good times'. As evolved as we are, part of our brain – the limbic system – still operates very much on a primitive level. It is easily startled, constantly worried, and has a propensity towards negativity. This mammalian, survival-based part of our brain will kick, scream and panic as it confuses spiritual surrendering with threats from harm. Ironically, letting go and yielding to what is often the only thing that works when you have exhausted all other options of pushing, wanting, worrying and fighting.

Sometimes a situation cannot resolve or heal itself until you fully release it to some unforeseeable force that is beyond your own perception. If you are struggling with an aspect of your life - or yourself - that you do not like, and you have exhausted all possible ways to change it but are getting nowhere, it may be time to try this practice: trusting that things will happen in the way they need to, when the time is ripe. As everything in nature, human life also goes through seasons and cycles. Perhaps it is not the time for a harvest yet. You would not ask a tree to be taller than it should be, a flower to be of a different colour, so why demand that of yourself?

## Exercise: the trust box

Here is a simple exercise that you can start today, to practise letting go and trusting life. It is inspired by the author Tosha Silver (2016), who puts all her anxiety-inducing problems, unresolved questions and worries into what she calls the 'God box'. In her practice, she writes her concerns on a piece of paper, slips it into the box and simply gives thanks for the perfect solution that is coming – even when she hasn't seen it yet.

This exercise is different from the standard cognitive behavioural technique 'the worry box' (which is useful in its own right). This takes it one step further in terms of spiritual development, and opens the door to a deeper state of equanimity that is beyond temporary relief. In essence, every piece of paper you put into the box becomes a vote of faith in life and in yourself. When done repeatedly, this practice helps to train and rewire your brain's existing neural pathways. You are using a ritual to teach your mammalian brain to calm down, and to gradually relinquish your need to know, to control and to push for the outcomes you want. Another added benefit of this practice is that, over the course of time you will have collected ample evidence of how things do usually get taken care of (this is often the case when you are given the benefit of an alternative time perspective). After a few weeks or months, when you review the box, even your rational, 'I will believe it when I see it' left brain will get a chance to catch up.

Learning to open to life will bring immediate and long-lasting benefits into your life. Ultimately, the goal is to align yourself with the belief that things are being done 'through you' rather than 'by you'. When you are freed from constant fears, worries and survival-based impulses, your brain will have the room to deal with what actually matters – your journey to self-actualization. Perhaps it is about being the best lover, parent, friend, person you can be; perhaps it is about being creative again; perhaps it is about reconnecting with your natural gifts and manifesting your full potential. With the ability to trust life comes not short-lived happiness nor hedonistic pleasures, but deep peace and lasting joy.

# Stepping into your truth

# Reclaiming authenticity

For how many years have you been trying to fit in, even when you don't? How much have you sacrificed, and how much discomfort have you endured, to be like everyone else?

Sometimes, your heart's strong pull and intensity may feel like a deficit or a burden – something you wish to be rid of. In trying to deny your own gifts, and your own voice, you might have become stuck in trying to prove to yourself and others how you can 'be normal' and be 'like everyone else'. *However, to be free, you must step into your truth: a place where, grounded in your uniqueness, you are confident in who you are.*

In this section, we will tackle the question of what it means to live freely and authentically as an emotionally sensitive, intense and gifted individual. Throughout history, many philosophers, theologians, social theorists and thinkers have explored the idea of authentic living. The existentialist philosopher Heidegger (1995), for instance, suggested that most of us live by way of quiet conformity to sooth our ultimate existential angst of being alone in this world. Without conscious examination, we naturally fall into living life according to the notion of an unnamed 'they;' we live as a 'they-self', and we do things simply because 'that is what one does'. Since working against the 'they-self' might mean we risk rejection and isolation, most people condition themselves to keep their heads down and play it safe. However, if we simply take on typical views of life and its rules and standards unquestioningly, eventually we too will come to believe that 'they' hold the truthful opinion about who we are. With our true selves numbed, we lose our vitality.

Being authentic means reclaiming oneself from unexamined conformity. Heidegger (1996) named the call for authenticity within ourselves the 'call of conscience', not in a moralistic sense, but because it is the ultimate responsibility of each one of us to realign our beings with our true selves and strip away the expectation placed upon us by the world outside. Living according to the unexamined, conformist way means that we are only numbing ourselves with a false sense of tranquillity – what existential psychologists call 'inauthentic tranquillity'. Because it is inauthentic, this 'tranquillity' is also fragile. That niggling feeling you get comes from something inside you searching for an answer, and your answer lies in the acknowledgement that you are a sensitive, intense and gifted person.

As humans, we all have a tendency to slip into seeing something and believing that it is what we want, even when it is not what our soul needs. D. H. Lawrence (1923) had this figured out when he said, 'Men are not free when they are doing just what they like... Men are only free when they are doing what the deepest self likes. And there is getting down to the deepest self! It takes some diving.' Because our most sincere self is buried inside, if we want to be free, we have to give up the illusion of doing what we 'think' we like, and seek what our soul wants, even when it is against the norm or places you in the minority.

Before now, you may have heard that 'authenticity takes courage'. Indeed, claiming authenticity – especially when it is an unconventional path – evokes a mixture of fear, loneliness and uncertainty. Taking this plunge is frightening at the start because it involves the 'killing off' of an old self. This process can be likened to that of death and rebirth, in which you have to let go of certain fantasies and expectations of what 'could have been'. It requires a radical stripping away of all that is out of alignment with your true path, meaning that certain relationships and ideas of who you are will be lost, and you may have to have a temporary period of isolation and emptiness before finding your new, true place in the world.

However, the sooner you step up, the sooner you will find that your fears dissipate. With courageously standing by your truth also comes a strong, compelling sense of clarity and relief and, at times, waves of bliss that come from knowing you are doing exactly the right thing. During those moments when you know you must take the leap, even when your cognitive mind fights against it, you also get to experience what it is like to be divinely guided by something bigger than yourself. Gradually, life will start to flow, and you will find it easier to make choices that may not be what you 'want' at the time, but what you know must be done.

You can only begin to heal from the wounds of being told you are 'too much' by fully acknowledging your identity as an emotionally intense gifted individual, and embracing your unique needs and desires, without holding back or apologizing. In the Hans Christian Andersen's story of the 'The Ugly Duckling', the main character does not have to 'do' anything to become heroic. From day one, there is nothing 'ugly' about the duckling, he is simply surrounded by characters who do not acknowledge his natural true self. The story is about him uncovering layers of wounds and coming into his own. Just like the ugly duckling, you might have believed that you ought to think, feel and behave like everyone else. Though it may seem 'safe' for a time, holding back your natural self in order to avoid criticism or to fit in will end up in nothing but the sickness of your soul. Ultimately, it is your birthright to be who you are, and to not go through life hiding, and it is within your power to rewrite the fictional account of yourself that for so long you thought was true. In essence, this is a process of reconnecting with the parts of yourself that you have shunned and disowned, and getting in touch with your deepest self.

For now, I hope you can find solace in the following excerpt from the original writing of Hans Christian Andersen, as he depicted the beautiful ending to the story of the duckling:

'It would be very sad, were I to relate all the misery and privations which the poor little duckling endured during the hard winter; but when it had passed, he found himself lying one morning in a moor, amongst the rushes. He felt the warm sun shining, and heard the lark singing, and saw that all around was beautiful spring.

Then the young bird felt that his wings were strong, as he flapped them against his sides, and rose high into the air.'

(Andersen, 1995)

### THE PATH TO CLAIMING YOUR AUTHENTIC IDENTITY
The following model outlines the various phases typically involved in coming to terms with one's true nature as a sensitive, intense and gifted person. This journey requires

you to consistently take steps to be more open, vulnerable and authentic with yourself and others. It calls for constant adjustment of your self-image and behaviour, so you can eventually find a balance between your values and the demands of society. Individual factors in your upbringing – from your immediate environment to your overarching culture – all affect how, and at what pace you move through these phases. Despite it looking like a linear model, finding and owning up to your true self is not a one-time event, but a life-long process, with no right or wrong path.

### ▶ Stage 1: Being unaware

At this point, you are completely unaware of your difference. You do not recognize your unique qualities – instead, you see yourself as a member of the mainstream population. With no reference point, you assume that everyone else thinks and feels as you do, and vice versa. While trying to behave like everyone else, you may repress any emerging internal thoughts and feelings that go against the cultural norm. However, since the traits of being sensitive and gifted are usually at least partly innate, you might already have a sense of 'being different' and have moved into phase two at a relatively young age.

### ▶ Stage 2: Becoming aware

Entering into this second stage, you begin to notice traits and qualities that set you apart from others. For instance, you find yourself exhibiting a great passion for certain subjects or causes, or experiencing infatuation to an extreme degree. As the depth of your emotions grows, you begin to actively question all aspects of who you are, from your personality type to your belief system. If your environment is not supportive towards individual gifts and standing out – such as in many cultures that value collectivism, conventions and sameness – you may become uncomfortable with your qualities. In addition, it is not uncommon for feelings of guilt, shame and fear of the unknown to come up. In response, you may learn to put up a 'false self', to stop or hide outward behaviours that reflect your natural excitabilities in order to blend in with your peers.

## ▶ Stage 3: Ambivalence and the development of a new self-narrative

In stage three, you begin to seek out information that explains your life experience. Through books, internet research, or other avenues, you may discover illuminating information about empaths, high sensitivity and giftedness. Your exploration will enable you to develop a new story of who you are and how you make sense of your life experiences. Your findings are not just eye-opening, but also healing, as you come to see that though you are in the minority, there are others like you.

Within your own heart, you may still walk a fine line between acceptance and rejection of your emotional intensity. Perhaps you come to accept part but not all of your true nature. You may decide that crying in a movie is acceptable, for instance, but feeling sentimental about a distant past is not. Part of you may still see your sensitive nature as something 'wrong' or 'selfish', and assure yourself that you will 'grow out' of it with time, medication or therapy.

You may dread the prospect of social alienation. Newly aware of the fact that others around you do not sense, feel or think the way you do, you begin to fear rejection by your family, peers and society at large. You may even feel guilty for being different and feel that you have betrayed those who raised you. As you start relating to others through your new self, you may still hit blockages stemming from low self-esteem, fear of exposure and internalized shame. If your relational experiences have been overwhelmingly negative, you might choose to reduce contact with the outside world, believing that your sensitivity means you cannot have a healthy social life. If you continue to suppress your true feelings in the damaging act of 'hiding and shrinking', you will end up with a sense of internal hollowness – not quite knowing who you are, and what your life purpose is.

As you awaken to your own emotional and empathic giftedness, you also come to see that life offers more possibilities than ever before – but embracing these opportunities will necessitate letting go of ideas and expectations that no longer serve you. Fear of the unknown – especially of others' rejection and envy – may cause you to shy away from your power. As Marianne Williamson's famous quote illustrates: 'Our deepest fear is not that we are inadequate. Our deepest fear is that we are powerful beyond measure. It is our light, not our darkness that most frightens us' (Williamson, 1992)

To progress into the next phase, you face the necessary task of embracing both your limitations and power and developing a new way of viewing yourself, revising your value system and making meaning out of life.

### ▶ Stage 4: Finding new alignments in the world

You begin to realize that owning up to your truth is not a static achievement, but a constant dance between your values, behaviours and how the world perceives you. As in previous stages, the questions of 'Whom do I trust?' or 'How much do I reveal about myself?' will linger. You tap into the perennial question of how to remain open and authentic without being naive in the world.

As you detach from the mainstream, you will become more discerning about who you surround yourself with. You now cherish quality, rather than quantity, of relationships. Supportive friendships or partnerships with those whose emotional depth matches yours are invaluable. Through virtual or actual communities, you can identify positive role models and begin to forge bonds that can start the process of healing the wounds whose origins lay in the relational world.

As you realize that you need not comply with society's standards of morality, love or success, you will be ready to re-negotiate your social and familial boundaries. Armed with the knowledge and assurance that you have the right to reduce contact with those who do not celebrate your unique qualities, your social circle may shift as you cut ties or move away from limiting relationships. This restructuring can reach beyond just social interaction. You may even feel compelled to change your living arrangements or occupation.

Increasingly, you will come to understand and trust that there is nothing fundamentally wrong with you. Such a realization sometimes brings about anger at what you've endured. To make good use of this energy and to advance into the next stage, you may transform it into an urge for positive changes in the world. Inspired by your story, you may feel compelled to stand up for those like you – those whose sensitive and gifted natures have led them to be pathologized or marginalized by society.

## ▶ Stage 5: Becoming real

At this juncture, you integrate what you have learned about yourself and your sensitive nature into a coherent self-identity. While embracing the fact that you are different, you can still appreciate and feel a deep, meaningful connection to the wider world.

By gaining emotional maturity, you can hold the tension between similarities and differences, between the desire to be unique and also to be part of a community. Despite the stigma, injustice and misunderstanding around sensitivity, you do not feel that the world is a battlefield between you and the 'non-sensitives'.

You also come to see your sensitivity as part of a whole – a piece of your identity – but not the summation of you. You see yourself as someone with a rich and dynamic personality – more than just a 'sensitive', 'intense' or 'gifted person'.

As a member of the world, confident in your identity, no longer will you need to put up a 'false self'. Though there will be situations where you can choose to reveal less of yourself, you will have found a safe space with a few trusted others to fully and freely be yourself – as intense, idealistic, driven and excited as you are.

Ideally, you will also be driven by a sense of purpose that is aligned with your gifts and have the inner strength to be a positive role model for other sensitive people. Through actively standing up for the issues you believe in, you will pave the way for other sensitive people to live and thrive in a world that can see them and celebrate their gifts.

# Exercise: taking the smallest next step forward

Where do you find yourself in the above model? Although presented as linear, in reality, the process is circular and zig-zagged. As you progress, you may find yourself going back and forth or even overlapping two or more phases at once.

Ask yourself: What is the next smallest step I can do, in the next 24 hours, towards owning my true self?

Moving towards authenticity requires a proactive and consistent stance to resolutely affirm your freedom of choice and to resist any tendency to be drowned out by the opinions of the majority. You do not have to start in a big and spectacular way. As Jeff Olson suggests in his book *The Slight Edge* (2013), it is small and consistent actions that make the most significant difference. A person who does this is using the power of compounding to make the biggest impact and change our lives for good.

Think about actions that would reaffirm your authenticity, such as saying no to a social engagement, expressing how you actually feel in a safe environment or allowing your intense passion for someone or something to be rather than suppressing it. Start with the smallest action possible. It may be as small as researching a certain topic. It is by breaking down your goal to the smallest piece, and starting there, that you gain the momentum to move forward.

Eventually, you may or may not be called to engage in actions on a larger scale. You may decide to tell your friends and family about what it means to be a sensitive and gifted person, to become a champion for those who are like you or even to engage in a humanitarian movement that would positively utilize your gift of empathy and passion. These are not necessary, however, for you to make an impact in the world. Just by showing up as your real self, you are allowing others to do the same.

In the end, the emotional realities behind your actions are more important than the actuality of what you do. Next time you fall prey to uncomfortable jealousy, remind yourself that, 'This is their life and not mine. I have my path.' Or, you can repeat the following quote from Oscar Wilde to yourself: 'Be yourself; everyone else is taken.' It may seem awkward and mechanical at first, but somehow your subconscious mind will receive your message. Becoming your authentic self is not an easy task, especially in the beginning, so you need to salute yourself on your courage and acknowledge that you are taking profound and necessary steps along the way.

In the coming chapters, we will look further at how to live an authentic life, and at some of the mindset shifts and small actions you can take towards it. Choosing your truth starts with a change in your awareness and way of being, which in turn affects how you approach the world in your daily activities. You reach congruence by being radically honest about what both your physical and feeling selves are telling you. It truly is a leap of faith but not a groundless one, as your passion and emotions solidly guide it.

# Staying in flow at work and in life

**WHEN THE NORMAL RULES DO NOT APPLY**

Positive psychologists define 'flow' as an 'optimal state of consciousness where we feel our best and perform our best' (Csíkszentmihályi, 1996). The idea of flow has long existed in human philosophy and spiritual traditions, and amongst many great thinkers, artists, and those who strive to live an optimal life. In the West, we call it being 'in the zone'. In his famous TED talk, *Flow, the Secret to Happiness*, Mihály Csíkszentmihályi (2004) described flow as a feeling of rapture. Since then, much more research has supported the flow state as a foundation for productivity, creativity and happiness.

To achieve a state of flow, we have to strike a balance between the level of our skills and the level of difficulty of the task at hand. Optimal performance is about finding that 'sweet spot' where your skill level matches the level of the challenge: if the task is too easy, you are likely to feel bored, empty or even depressed. If the task is too challenging, you will be held back by anxiety. Neither of these cases leads to flow.

The theory itself sounds straight forward, yet finding your sweet spot as an intense person can be a complicated issue. If your 'natural requirement' for challenges and stimulation deviates from that of the norm, others will be surprised by, or even feel intimidated by your lifestyle choices. Without sufficient self-knowledge and a solid sense of self, it is easy to be swayed by other people's opinions and end up feeling confused about how to live your life.

With your gifted perception, you naturally see and feel what others don't, and this is manifested in various aspects of your life. Emotionally, you feel passion and romance intensely. Sometimes, you may express your feelings and need for intimacy way before the other person is ready. Intellectually, you can get excited about various subjects and have such expansive curiosity and drive for learning, that others cannot keep up with the breadth and depth of your knowledge. Sensually, you may derive such intense pleasure from experiences, that you can hardly contain yourself. For a long time, you probably wondered why others don't see what you see and feel what you feel.

To achieve optimal performance and quality of life, your baselines of psychological, emotional and physical needs ought to be met by your lifestyle choices – from the length of time you wish to engage in intellectual debates, to the hours you work or sleep, to the kind of relationships you have with people. Finding your flow is especially challenging if you have advanced abilities or heightened intensities because 'common sense' or 'general rules' do not apply in your case. For instance, you may need a higher level of intellectual complexity in your work to not feel lethargic and empty, thus attending lectures in the evenings, even after a long day of work, may be nourishing for you. Perhaps your idea of fun is not the same as others'. Another example is that you need to be much more physically active to stay energized, and often you fidget, not because you are anxious but because your environment under-stimulates you. Having these intensities does not mean you are 'better' or more superior in any way, as you may well be limited in other aspects, such as not being able to sit still or concentrate for long hours.

Here are some of the strategies that may help you to find your own 'sweet spot' for optimal performance, both at work and in life.

### ▶ 1 Cultivate a close relationship with yourself

The path to optimizing your performance at work is as unique as your fingerprint.

To know your most authentic and unique needs, you must cultivate a close relationship with yourself. You will have to develop the ability to self-reflect. Perhaps you can think of yourself as an investigator, be consistently curious about your internal states, and carefully observe how various activities, environments, and people affect you. Try to take notes or keep a mental record of how you do in different circumstances. You can also start a mindfulness practice, or a reflective journal, to practise being introspective.

### ▶ 2 Screen out 'noises of the masses'

As an intense person, it is essential that you learn to screen out 'noises of the masses'. Your needs are different from those that 'common sense' suggests. Be especially mindful of criticism or commentaries such as 'That is too much', 'You need to rest', or 'I cannot believe you just did that'. Traditional wisdom is not always correct; philosophers call this 'appeal to common practice' – the false assumption that 'this is right because we have always done it this way'. Always evaluate when someone tells you 'you need to…'; no matter how well-intentioned they are, no one has full access to your unique physical and mental make-up, desires and aspirations.

In reality, you do not have to put out what you like or do for public judgement. You do not have to publicize your insights or broadcast your preferences. All you have to do is to preserve the part of you that is curious about all information that comes your way and sees the world as presenting to you a series of learning opportunities. You are free to disregard everything that does not fit.

### ▶ 3 Be honest and compassionate about your limitations

Authenticity is about 'letting go of who you wish to be, to become who you are'. In the process of finding your ideal blueprint for an optimal life, you will come face to face with your limits. Being self-compassionate is the courageous act of meeting yourself exactly as you are – no more and no less.

Committing to an honest, but self-compassionate attitude will give you the patience and intelligence to find your place without drowning in other people's opinions.

### ▶ 4 Extend your comfort zone sometimes

While being honest about your limitations is important, a life devoid of stimulation is not a fulfilling one. To find your level of peak performance, you need to continuously raise the challenge – either by diversifying or deepening the practice of what you do. In *The Rise of Superman* (2014), flow specialist Steven Kotler suggests the 4 per cent rule: the challenge should be 4 per cent greater than your existing skill level. These small increments put your body and mind in the zone for optimal focus and learning. In other words, you have to get out of your comfort zone to find your zone.

### ▶ 5 Reclaiming your curiosity

As a gifted person, you are naturally curious and inquisitive. However, we live in a society that encourages cynicism and is often quick to disregard curiosity as naivety. As we have become fearful of appearing foolish, we have trained ourselves to refrain from openness. Modern education encourages critical thinking, yet with it come the unhelpful byproducts of hyper-criticism and cynicism. This can be observed in all aspects of our lives, from reality TV to the way we socialize, where almost nothing seems to pass without a hint of sarcasm. See if you can reflect on the last time you held back from excitement and curiosity due to the fear of appearing foolish.

## Exercise: back to the classroom

To reconnect with your natural love of knowledge and learning, make a list of ten questions you would like answered – either as a child or as an adult. It could be anything, from secrets of the universe to how to make a perfect cake. Then make some time to solve the puzzles, enjoying the process of discovery as best you can. As you explore, don't forget this mantra: 'Stay hungry, stay foolish' (the title of a book by Rashmi Bansal, made famous by Steve Jobs quoting it in his 2005 commencement speech at Stanford).

The art of finding your flow is an intricate process and will involve some trial-and-error. It is nonetheless a worthwhile endeavour that has the potential to greatly enhance the sense of meaning and quality of your life. You do not have to be 'there' already, you are already at your healthiest when you keep your mind open, recognize your gifts and virtues, and proactively strive towards becoming the best version of yourself.

## Excercise: pruning away the 'shoulds'

The first step to finding what holds you back from authenticity is to identify the 'shoulds' in your life. Many of us are plagued by these 'should' or 'shouldn't' beliefs that are born out of other people's limited understanding of who we are. These 'should' beliefs are sometimes subtle and sometimes loud. Often they come from the outside world, but sometimes they are what we have internalized. Whenever you listen to the 'should' rather than your gut feeling, you are living for others rather than yourself. Though they may feel easy, familiar and like the obvious thing to do, choices based on 'should' are a long way from joy, deep fulfilment, and the sense of awe that you can feel as an authentic-living intense person.

Here is a quick exercise to help you start discovering and pruning away the 'should' and 'shouldn't' beliefs that do not deserve a place in your life.

1 Take out your journal, and create a time and a space for this exercise.
2 Start to write down as many of the 'should' and 'shouldn't' belief statements you can think of. If you don't know where to begin, it is often useful to think about a current challenge in your life. Are you facing a particular dilemma or decision point? What would be some of the 'should' and 'shouldn't' beliefs associated with that? An example may be: 'I want to leave my job now but I shouldn't because that would be irresponsible'.
3 Now, let's dig deeper into your subconscious thought processes by identifying the reasoning behind your statements. Try to complete your sentences using the word 'because'. For instance, 'I should go to this party even when I don't want to because (I believe that is what it means to be a good friend)', or, 'I should stay in this relationship because (I have made a commitment)'.

4   Then, see if you can identify any higher personal values and principles behind your reasoning. Your personal value system should involve a set of virtues that you see as important to you. Some examples are kindness, honesty, loyalty, creativity and autonomy. Virtues are an essence of your character, and you feel most at ease when your actions are aligned with your most valued qualities. For instance, you may say: 'I should stay in this relationship because I have made a commitment, and one of my virtues is loyalty.' Ideally, your beliefs about what you should and should not do are supported by the principles and values that mean something to you. Now, when you have to complete the should/shouldn't statement with an empty rationale such as 'because this is what people do', or 'because this is the way it is', examine it further. This is when you discover beliefs that you have imported from the outside world, but that are not necessarily congruent to your own, unique set of values.

5   Choose from one of the beliefs identified in Step 4, then ask yourself: Is this absolutely true? How do I know that it is? When, from whom and how have I come to learn it? Work through them one by one. You may take some time to travel back into the past, to investigate the origins of these beliefs, and to examine their relevance to your life now.

6   Now, for just three minutes, experiment with how you feel on the inside, both emotionally and physically, when you drop that should/shouldn't belief. Take a slow, attentive and meditative stance, and toy with the idea. This does not mean you need to take any immediate action or make any changes, so relax. The purpose of this exercise is simply to warm up your mind, and to slowly make room for new possibilities.

7   Try to imagine how life would be different without these particular 'should' or 'shouldn't' beliefs. Since it is likely that you have never contemplated a different life path outside of the one you are living, this step may create some anxiety. See if you can approach it lightly and playfully. Contemplate the following: what different choices would I have made if I did not have this belief? How might things be different? Where might I be? What would I be doing? See if you can create a vivid image in your mind.

8   Make some notes in your journal about this experience. You do not have to decide whether or not you drop the should/shouldn't beliefs right here and now. Simply allow any insights to come to you, and trust that the necessary changes will occur to you when the timing is right.

# Expressing your true self safely

As an emotionally gifted person, you have a unique way of being in and seeing the world. Across history, it has always been the emotionally gifted creative visionaries who tell and give people what they do not know they want yet. However, individuals who have something different to say are often ridiculed.

Emotionally gifted people cannot stand a facade for long. They often have a strong will to know the truth and to tell it. Since you also have an intense sense of justice and unwavering passion for life, it is inevitable that you ask the supposedly 'dangerous' questions, and scratch the surface to reach a deeper level of knowledge and understanding. Naturally, anywhere you find yourself, you challenge the status quo, which makes you vulnerable to resentment and reprisals from those who feel intimidated. Telling the truth, even when not directed at anyone, still serves to 'expose' those who are not ready to see it or to do something about it. Just by pointing out the hypocrisies in the situation, you are questioning the current reality that everyone else has been riding along with. Nobody likes that, and that is why Galileo was attacked when he first pointed out that the world was not flat.

As a result of being ridiculed or silenced as a child, you might have learned with great pain, to shut up, to keep your head down and to suppress your voice. Always feeling and knowing deep down that you are different, that you don't fit in, that your natural self is often received with fear, apathy or even hostility, you might have learned to hide and shrink your voice. This is terribly unfortunate as your vision and perception are often the seeds for progression in our world, as well as a reflection of the highest integrity. The situation is as author Anthon St Maarten poignantly puts it: 'Being the soothsayer of the tribe is a dirty job, but someone has to do it'. Even though you may not recognize yourself as a particularly brave person, the fact that you are different from the norm means that to survive in this world, you have no choice but to develop extra skills, resilience and courage.

One of the most valuable life lessons that will continue to benefit the emotionally sensitive and intense person, is to find the balance between being the wild, free and real you, and staying safe from judgements and attacks in this world. While it is important to live authentically and express yourself fully and freely, you also need to know when and how to adapt to live in harmony with others. It is in knowing how to be your true self – with all the intensities, enthusiasm, and deep passion for the truth, yet maintaining adequate boundaries so that you can preserve your vitality and safely navigate unpredictable and sometimes hostile social situations.

## ASSESSING THE CONTEXT WISELY AND ADAPTING ACCORDINGLY

Some environments are safer for the emotionally gifted than others.

For instance, in work settings, families and cultures where individualism is valued, or in countries and cities where there is high social and geographic mobility, differences are tolerated. In contrast, in collectivist cultures and groups where sameness is emphasised, and conflicts are avoided, the individual self is usually subordinated to the interests of surface harmony. However, no matter how open a culture, people still have a tendency to dislike or reject what is unfamiliar.

It is therefore important to assess each situation and context carefully and manage your expectations of other people's degree of openness towards your intensity. For instance, in a conservative workplace environment, it is wise to pause and assess before exposing your revolutionary ideas or diving in with your unrestrained passionate self. This act is not about hiding, suppressing, or denying yourself but rather finding a mature and strategic way to bring your gifts into the world.

Having different personas – social faces you present to the world – is not 'bad'. As adults, we all have different roles in different settings. In fact, being able to adapt to diverse groups and settings, and be at ease and familiar with each side of yourself, is a vital part of being a healthy adult. Sometimes, it is wise to consider how best to fit in like 'an Englishman in New York'.

You can also use your imagination in inescapable situations where you have to hold yourself back. You can pretend that you are an actor or actress playing a role, or you may imagine yourself going in wearing a 'uniform'. You can go into these settings knowing that, at the end of the day, when you are back in a safe environment, you can take your uniform off, and fully embrace the real you – passionate, gifted, wholehearted and courageous. This way you can protect your real self from any unnecessary attacks or bullying, and preserve your authentic spirit.

## MINDING YOUR NEED TO BE SEEN AND HEARD

The emotionally gifted person sometimes lets their intensity and excitement get the better of them. This is a natural expression of their exuberance and speedy perceptive and processing powers.

However, overexposure is sometimes driven by a deep, unfulfilled need to be seen and heard. It is human nature to want to be acknowledged; being deprived of the attention, appreciation and affirmation you had needed as a child might have left a gaping hole in you. At times, you may be overcome by a compelling, almost irrational desire to be acknowledged, praised and valued. You may tell your story, or voice your opinion, regardless of whether or not the setting is appropriate. When your action feels compulsive, frustrating and needy, you know it is coming from the wounded child within you. If you end up sharing your deep feelings and psychological insights with those who are not ready to receive them, you might be met with reactions ranging from blank stares and perplexity, to unease and rejection. Sadly, as adults it is harder to get our emotional needs met, since being an adult automatically means we take on a different role in a group and people have different expectations of us. When you are in unfamiliar surroundings such as a new workplace, you may have to remind the part of you that yearns to be seen and heard to be patient.

The trick is to be mindful of your deep emotional needs, and to ensure that you satisfy them as you interact with people who are able to accept you for yourself. You may summon a trusted group of friends, a counsellor, a close friend or an intimate partner that you can trust. If possible, identify 'your people'.

You may not be able to find one person or one group that can meet all your needs, but you can get your different needs met in different places. For instance, you can be fully excited by finding people with the same 'obsession' and desires as you have. You may identify other equally intense and sensitive individuals with whom you could share the deep feelings, moments of awe, and the tenderness of being a sensitive person inhabiting this space. When it is safe to do so, reveal your gifted self to the trusted others, but see your openness and vulnerability as true offerings, not merely as ways to get your needs met.

## CHANNELLING YOUR GIFTS INTO CREATIVE PURSUITS

One the most productive ways of using your unique gifts, passion and insights, is to channel them through creative means. If those in your immediate circle do not rejoice in your company, appreciate your unique offerings, or share your insights and deep feelings, you can share them with the world. You can skilfully channel your need to be seen and heard into artistic pursuits.

Sharing your insights and feelings with the wider world – a much bigger audience – is, paradoxically, safer than trying to get your voice heard in a small group. You are simply going in with the pure intention of being authentic, and you are not forcing anyone to see or accept you. All you are doing is revealing your truest self in the hope that those on your frequency level – and even those not on your frequency level – will in time, get to hear your message. With the internet, there are no geographical boundaries to how far your message can reach. People who need to hear you will come from far and wide, because there are no holds barred; no one feels trapped, coerced or engulfed. They are free to come and join you in your virtual tribe, or they can walk away if what they hear from you makes them uncomfortable.

The way to authentic expression involves overcoming your internalized shame, coming out from hiding, and feeling confident and loving towards your natural self again. You can loosen the grip that fear has on you by allowing courage and positive actions to take charge, by testing new waters, and by stepping onto bigger playing fields. Most importantly, do not let others' inability to appreciate your true self to send you back into hiding, or retreating into your shell. When attacks happen, see all insults, humiliation and disappointment as launch pads to propel you further in the advancement of your skills and originality. This quest will ultimately lead you to a place in this world where you are not just tolerated but celebrated.

### Reflection prompts

To find a way of living in this world as an intense and emotionally sensitive person is not a linear process. Sometimes, as you try, it feels like you take two steps forward and three steps back. During the course of finding your place, you may overstep boundaries, or get hurt, and need to return to the safety zone you are trying to get away from. But each time you are pushed back, you re-emerge more robust, and with a clearer idea of who you are. You get to refine your self-acceptance concept and even re-define who you are, your role and your way of being in this world. In the end, it is a balancing act. It is about matching the Yin and the Yang, the assertiveness and the patience, speaking up versus simply observing, and individuality versus harmony. Sometimes you need to stretch to get out of your comfort zone, to know your limits and to challenge them. And it is through this gradual and rocky process of going back and forth, holding the tension between uncertainty and safety, and taking one small step at a time, that you find your boundary and eventually find balance.

Find the time and space to be with your journal. Sitting comfortably, bring your awareness to your breathing. Then ask yourself the following questions:

1 Where in my life do I hide and shrink in fear?

2 Paradoxically, where in my life do I reveal too much of myself, too soon, when it is not in my own or anyone else's best interest to do so?

3 Do I have a need to be seen and heard that comes from unhealed wounds from childhood?

4 Where and when is it wise to hold back for a bit?

5 So far, how have I been approaching these situations (school, work, meeting someone new), and has this changed over the years, based on my experience?

6 Do I have friends, a partner, or a trusted other with whom I can be completely free and authentic?

7 Do I have a channel for my creative insights and revolutionary ideas?

# Letting authenticity take charge

## A MINDSET SHIFT

Authenticity is the practice of letting go of who we think we *should* be and embracing who we *are*. This step is undeniably profound, though it may seem like nothing more than a subtle mental shift. Such a shift in perspective is radical: when things 'fall away' from your life, instead of fighting against it, you examine how they might not belong in the first place. For example, if being stuck in a certain job role makes you sick – to the point where you can no longer sustain your position – instead of being critical of yourself or focusing on the loss, you can choose to view this as a 'dropping away' initiated by your most authentic self. Although the feelings around an apparent loss might be painful, you have also now made space for something else, something more aligned with your natural desires and capabilities.

One of the challenges many sensitive individuals face is determining what to keep and what to let go of in life, in order to avoid becoming over-burdened by responsibilities and unnecessary stimuli. This is when authenticity can be so useful: when you are just being yourself – that is, not stretching beyond your limits nor trying to be who you are not – you will naturally filter out the bad apples in your life and attract people and opportunities that are the best natural fit for you.

This makes the path to success and happiness a lot simpler: instead of twisting yourself to fit into a certain mould, you only have to focus on being as honest as you can be. By doing so, certain things, people and situations that no longer serve you – even if part of you thinks that they are what you want or need – will drop away. You may need to temporarily grieve these losses, yet when you are able to commit to trusting the process, you will gain a sense of deep equanimity in regard to people and relationships.

Next time you feel rejected or abandoned, keep in mind that relationships are always a dance and never one-sided. View events and relationships in life as following a natural order: two people gravitate towards each other, may come to walk a path with each other and learn from each other, and then, when that ceases to serve them, the journey comes to a natural end, resulting in them moving apart. With practice, you will begin to see that all things – people, places, jobs – are just like atoms in the universe, or elements in nature. They are constantly coming together and falling away, and it is a process that is not personal to you. Eventually, integration with your true self will leave you with a particular vibration discernible to others like you.

To allow this practice of authentic discernment to serve you, you must have faith in its power as a natural 'filter'. When you allow yourself to be guided by your honest truth, the right people and opportunities will gravitate towards you. Increasingly, you will come to know and accept your unique traits: your strengths, weaknesses and preferences. You will be the champion of your authentic self, a guardian of your self-esteem, and a guide to set for yourself healthy boundaries with others. Consider the following quote by Margaret Young:

> 'Often people attempt to live their lives backwards: they try to have more things, or more money, in order to do more of what they want so that they will be happier. The way it actually works is the reverse. You must first be who you really are, then do what you really need to do, in order to have what you want.'
>
> Margaret Young (in Breathnach, 2011)

When combined with a sense of trust, you can count on your authenticity to lead you to abundance in all areas of your life by acting as a natural filter.

# Exercise: looking inwards for your truth

Authenticity is actualized by a careful process of looking inwards. As your truth is made up of your convictions, urges, desires, points of pain and passion, you can get to know your authentic self by becoming intimate with your own psychological and physiological processes. For the next week, set an intention to closely monitor your feelings and energy levels, moment by moment, and listen to yourself as if your life depended on it, letting yourself be guided by where your energy goes. Then, at the end of the week, ask yourself the following questions:

1  What have I learned about myself by looking inwards to explore the signals and messages from my physical body and my emotions?

2  What brings me joy and what brings me pain?

3  How do my sensitivity and intensity make me different, so that 'common sense', or the 'normal approach' do not work for me?

4  Are there situations or relationships in which I have been contorting myself in order to make them work?

5  What is the one thing that I can release now, to honour my sensitivity, intensity and integrity?

6  What if all that I thought was 'wrong' was actually 'right'?

7  Where in my life can I allow my honest truth to be a natural filter?

If you have recently lost something – a person, a status, a job, an opportunity – repeat the following affirmation, either out loud or in writing:

> 'Even though I am not yet aware of where this is leading, even though it pains me to have to let go of ..., I am open to the possibility that it is more aligned with my deeper truth. This is an opportunity for me to train my mental flexibility, and to adopt a wider perspective. Perhaps my discomfort is a growing pain.
>
> As I now begin to remember the truth of who I am, I give myself permission to let go, so I can make space for something that is truer to who I am.'

# Being in the world

# Looking after your emotional boundaries

As an emotionally gifted person, your natural tendency is to give, to love and to share. From a young age, you have been acutely aware of your own pain, and the pain of others, and have had a deep desire to alleviate suffering for the greater good of humanity. As a result of your empathic gifts, you may attract a lot of people coming to you for advice and comfort. With some, you leave the exchange feeling inspired, empowered and resourceful, but with others, you are left exhausted, as if they have dumped their emotional baggage onto you. Sometimes, you are left feeling sad, attacked, or even ashamed and guilty, without knowing why.

As someone who is empathically gifted, you emit an empathic vibrational energy that is rare in today's world; this energy can attract others who wish to use it to complete something that is lacking in themselves. A concept in psychoanalytic psychology known as 'projective identification' can help us understand this phenomenon. Projective identification is a manoeuvre that often goes hand in hand with toxic envy, in which a person 'dumps' their 'bad' feelings and qualities onto others. You know you have been the recipient of projective identification when you are suddenly seized by an intense feeling that you were not expecting to have (Ogden, 1979).

It is worth pointing out that the person who attacks you is likely acting out from the less evolved aspects of themselves, so their rational self may not be aware of the primitive driving forces behind their destructive behaviours. Often, the projector uses the manoeuvre to get rid of unwanted feelings such as envy and inferiority. They may assume the position of the superior, and disown as well as project onto you these unwanted aspects of themselves. You will then feel the impact of these negative projections – such as the feeling of inferiority or shame. Being the 'recipient' of projective identification is very unpleasant, confusing and difficult to bear; it is an infiltration of the mind and body, which can even, sometimes, be felt physically. These processes are insidious and seep in slowly, and it can be tough to distinguish between what is yours and what is the result of the projector's 'dumping' (Curtis, 2015).

If you can tune into your intuitive abilities, your physical and emotional selves will be able to guide you. Instinctively, you are aware that some relationships drain you more than they nourish you; you know what it is like when you walk into a room, and the energy feels wrong, and you know what it is like to be stuck in a negative loop with someone who is energetically demanding. But many of us have learned to disconnect from or distrust our precious inner guide. It is hard to listen to our intuition when we live in a world that does not talk about what it means to be hyper-empathic. No one has ever told you about what it is like to pick up on other people's implicit anger, or warned you of the impact of toxic emotional transfer. Thus, when you are caught in an unhealthy interaction and feel bad, you might think: 'I am too sensitive, I think too much'. When your default position is to believe that there is something wrong with you, you miss out on the important warning signs of boundary violations.

Your emotional boundaries mark an invisible force field that regulates your interaction with other people. If you fail to recognize it when you have become the target of others' psychic attacks or 'emotional dumping', your emotional boundaries will be compromised. Most boundary trespasses are not immediately recognizable. You might be left feeling violated and psychologically abused before you know it. If you have not honed your empathic skills and balanced them with robust and healthy boundaries, you could eventually become burnt out.

Getting to know your vulnerabilities is an empowering first step in keeping you safe in the social world, and safeguarding yourself against those who may exploit your gifts. First of all, let's review some of the reasons why you may be prone to emotional boundary trespass.

### ▶ 1 You assume the best in others

Many emotionally gifted people are naturally trusting; you have an idealistic nature, a strong sense of justice, and hold yourself to a high moral standard of behaviour. It may not occur to you that others are less idealistic than you are and that people can be petty, jealous and insecure. As a child, you might not have fully understood why others did not share your views of what the world should look like, or you were surprised to learn that anyone could act out of toxic envy or resentment (see also Chapter 6).

If instead of seeing the origins of other people's criticisms and attacks clearly, you have internalized the mistreatment and skewed perceptions that were projected onto you, you may end up with the belief that the faults lie in you, and you become vulnerable to shame, guilt and a negative self-image. You may also begin to distrust your inner reality and disregard what your gut sense tells you.

### ▶ 2 It is not always obvious

Often, bullies attack out of insecurity and fear, although they are not themselves aware of what drives them. One of the most insidious and destructive social dynamics that the emotionally intense and gifted can be impacted by is toxic envy.

Essentially, envy is about an inability to bear the reality that life is not always fair. This is why envy is especially pronounced in the realm of natural talents and attributes – when the envied person seems to possess qualities which are given and cannot be bought or even earned through hard work. Most people are reluctant to acknowledge their destructive envy, as it often leads to intense guilt and shame.

Envy, and its twin emotion *Schadenfreude*, are natural occurrences in the human psyche, yet most people deny them or remain unaware of their impact. Borrowed from the German language, *Schadenfreude* is the pleasure derived from the misfortune of others. The person experiencing it will feel joy at seeing or hearing about the troubles and failures of others.

Both envy and *Schadenfreude* are biologically-based emotions, but the reality can be obscured since most people will go to almost any lengths to cover them up. Research studies using fMRI brain scans show that individuals are unwilling to admit to such feelings or are simply not consciously aware of them. Even when people are aware of their envy, they automatically generate rationalizations to justify the actions they want to take. Since a lot of negative emotions, dumping and psychological attacks happen on a subtle and subconscious level, both the attacker and the attacked may not be aware of it happening.

### ▶ 3 You are busy making sure that you are the best you can be

Being a seeker of truth – 'getting to the bottom of things' – is a profound need for many emotionally gifted people. You like to assess a situation thoroughly, using all the available information, and to make sure that you have behaved in a way that is congruent with your values and standards. This urge to thoroughly evaluate is especially compelling when it comes to matters involving your character and integrity. When negative events happen, instead of defending yourself, you are likely to focus on making sure that you have done your best and knew the 'truth' as far as you possibly could. You may endlessly analyse others' negative opinions of you unless you can prove that what they say is wrong. In doing so, you may also take on too much responsibility for what has happened, without acknowledging the part played by the other parties and by various external factors.

### ▶ 4 You have learned to disown your power

Perhaps you were shut down by parents looking to curb your natural excitement and exuberance. Or, as a child, you were told that showing or using your capabilities may make others feel bad and that you must hide them. If you were cast into the role of the 'sick' or 'wrong' one, and had your emotional gifts condemned or pathologized, you may also fear – consciously or unconsciously – that you will be punished if you stand up for yourself. Over time, you have learned to invalidate your own world views, feelings and hunches. You do not feel that you are allowed to 'take up space', be assertive or fight back when your rights are violated. You feel unable to exercise your healthy anger and, as a result, it takes you a long time to recognize boundary trespass, when others are overstepping the mark.

### ▶ 5 Your compassion overrides the need for self-protection

Being emotionally sensitive goes together with being empathetic and compassionate. It is your second nature to see and feel the pain and suffering of others beneath the facade they have put up. Even when you are on the receiving end of their attacks and projections, you see the vulnerabilities behind bullies' behaviours. Rather than defending yourself, you see past the pain that is being inflicted upon you.

While your compassionate nature, coupled with the intention to move towards forgiveness, is tremendously valuable, it must not be confused with the act of 'bypassing', or prematurely jumping to forgiveness, as a way of evading painful feelings such as hurt and anger. You know this is happening when you catch yourself avoiding the necessary confrontation, or talking around an insulting event in a distant, third-person manner. You may suppress your anger by not registering the injustice of the situation. You may also rationalize the event and find excuses for others' behaviours. However, you can't be truly compassionate without first becoming emotionally honest with yourself and acknowledging the natural reactions of pain and resentment. Although it is saddening to know that others can attack you out of their own insecurities and vulnerabilities, it is important that you see reality as it is, rather than internalizing the negative messages that come your way.

In the end, you can only act productively and be a gift to the world if you prioritize taking care of your authentic emotional needs. If you feel unfairly treated, bullied or ridiculed by those around you, rather than rationalizing or diminishing your pain, see if you can be a kind but solemn observer. You can notice and contain all the complex phenomena and emotions that arise in the situation – including their pain, your pain, the conflicts, the fears and frustration in both of you. It is only when you can be gentle, honest and loving towards yourself, that your gifts and your love can flow to those around you.

When we are bullied, put down or repeatedly oppressed, our normal, human response is anger. Anger is a useful emotion that prompts us to set our boundaries and to claim our power.

However, if you grew up in a childhood environment that prohibited or suppressed anger expressions, owning anger can become a challenge for you.

As children, we need to know that it is okay to feel angry and that there is a healthy way of expressing it. Even when mistreated, all children naturally try to protect their relationship with their caregivers, even if this means suppressing their anger or turning it towards themselves. This is because, for vulnerable young children, to be mad at the people they depend on feels unsafe. If you were not allowed to express your feelings freely or to stand up for yourself, you might have become locked in the habit of blaming yourself for the actions and wrongdoing of others.

Being able to relate to healthy anger is essential in maintaining our emotional boundaries. When we drop our boundary-protecting anger and ignore our needs and wishes, we get into a vulnerable self-abandoning position that is prone to violations.

If you have been suppressing anger for a long time, you may have developed a fear around it. Although acknowledging others' aggression towards you can be unpleasant, without sobering up to reality and learning to exercise your healthy anger, your boundaries will continue to be compromised.

The following exercise will guide you through a process of reconnecting to this emotion.

## Exercise: reconnecting with healthy anger

Find a comfortable position in which to be with your journal, then bring your awareness to your breathing. Without trying to change it, simply notice it. Allow your shoulders and abdomen to soften.

1 Start by bringing up a small incident that irritated you. Notice how you experience anger in your body – it may come up as heat, a sensation, or a subtle movement within you. You may wish to make a sound that represents how you feel – anything from 'Argh!' to a swear word.

**2** Here is a list of sentences. Try to complete them as spontaneously as possible – don't overthink it. Do not edit as you write, as there is no right or wrong answer. Words and thoughts may not immediately emerge. See if you can, for just a few minutes, turn off your internal censor, and allow your thoughts and feelings to flow naturally on the page.

✳ The last time I felt angry was when…
✳ When I feel anger, what I usually do is…
✳ I have been doing this since…
✳ For me, anger is…
✳ I felt most angry as a child when…
✳ If I could turn the clock back, I would change…
✳ Now as an adult the way I deal with anger is…
✳ As I stay open to my anger, I notice that I am…

Aim not to suppress, but to welcome and channel your anger. Notice how, if you allow the energy to flow through you, it can be invigorating, rather than depressing. Remind yourself that it is safe to feel it, as it will soon pass and simply feeling the feeling is not going to cause any harm. You do not have to let it overwhelm you, and you do not have to do anything with it. All you are doing in this exercise is to honour your feelings, without hurtful expressions or repressions, and without harming yourself or others.

We begin to find grace and strength in our experiences when we give up being passive victims of circumstance, and honestly ask: 'What can I make of what happened? How can I work with this event so that it opens me to something new? How can this serve me and others?'

When your anger flows freely, it will help you maintain your boundaries, your inner convictions and a sense of healthy detachment from things around you. Having a healthy relationship with anger will allow you to access a stable sense of self, and to tap into your inner strengths.

# Understanding passive-aggressive behaviour

All relationships and their dynamics involve two parties, but many emotionally intense and sensitive people can take too much responsibility for what happens, without recognizing the role of the other person involved.

Interactions and relationships with certain people are particularly draining and energy sapping – usually, not because they maliciously did something, but because of their own limitations in handling emotions in a mature way. Being in unhealthy or co-dependent relationships with such people can tremendously drain your physical and emotional resources; due to the unconscious dynamic, they can leave you feeling irritated, manipulated, guilty or even ashamed, without you knowing why.

In this section, we will learn about one of the most common, yet insidious forms of emotional boundary trespass – passive-aggressive behaviour.

As an emotionally sensitive person, it is important that you recognize such behaviour when it comes your way, in order to safeguard your emotional health.

### WHAT IS PASSIVE-AGGRESSIVE BEHAVIOUR?

Passive-aggressive behaviour is the use of passivity and covert strategies in dealing with one's own needs and wants in a relationship. People who are passive-aggressive fail to own up to their own thoughts and emotions, and can only express their negative and unwanted feelings and qualities by projecting them outwards, rather than processing them internally.

Passive-aggressive disorder was once considered a form of personality disorder and was included in the *Diagnostic and Statistical Manual of Mental Disorders*. However, since experts recognize that passive-aggression is a common phenomenon even amongst those without mental illness, it was edited out of the diagnostic manual.

Here, the term 'passive-aggressive people' is (over-simplistically) used to refer to those who use passive-aggressive behaviour as a predominant way of coping within interpersonal relationships. Despite the arbitrary nature of the language, my intention here is not to put people in boxes or to define a certain group as 'the passive-aggressive type' in a black-or-white manner.

We all use passive-aggression as a way of dealing with our anger from time to time. It only becomes problematic when it becomes a default unconscious and rigid way of being. People who are passive-aggressive may not behave that way all the time, but it is frequent enough that it becomes toxic to themselves and those around them.

Recognizing someone as being passive-aggressive is not a clear-cut process. Here are some of the most observable signs:

► Rather than directly expressing their needs and wants, they withdraw their time, support, resources and attention. This includes prolonged silent treatment.

► They may intentionally underperform, fail to meet certain demands or shirk agreed responsibilities. They may claim that they are unable, rather than unwilling, to do certain things. For instance, they may limit their contributions to shared responsibilities, such as work projects, household chores, or functional communication.

► Passive-aggressiveness can also be exhibited in a 'circuitous' way – which means they express their opposition or distaste in an indirect manner using procrastination, dawdling, intentional forgetfulness and inefficiency. They may claim innocence and make you feel like you are the demanding one (Millon and Radovanov, 1995).

► They are constantly grumpy and moody, but rather than explaining or owning up to their mood swings, they leave you to 'guess' what is going on.

► They use trivial complaints as a way of expressing their discontent – complaining about little things so that they don't have to express the full extent of their resentment.

- During conflicts, they can instantly shut down. When they feel attacked, they get defensive and reply sharply with 'fine', 'whatever' and so on.

- They may simply evade difficult situations or 'disappear' in the middle of a conflict.

- They use sarcasm and humour as a way of putting you down, claiming that they are 'just teasing'.

- They express violence indirectly – such as hitting the wall, slamming doors or harming themselves.

Other signs of passive-aggressive behaviour may be more subtle and not immediately recognizable. For instance, in day-to-day interactions, it is not uncommon for a passive-aggressive person to never show initiative. They may not even be able to state their preference most of the time. This is because asserting any thing will demand the kind of energy they can't muster. And making a decision requires the willingness to be accountable for its consequences.

Interactions with someone who acts passive-aggressively leave you drained because most of the time you are not interacting with someone who is emotionally mature. They are not willing to take responsibility for their actions, hold ownership for their feelings, or be accountable for the consequences of their choices. Even if on the surface they seem able to manage 'adult responsibilities', when things become difficult, they have a tendency to dodge accountability and cover up their true feelings. In many ways, they are psychologically and emotionally dependent, and it is their infantile tendencies that leave people around them feeling tired and confused.

Even when they are not directing their passive anger at you, being in a close relationship with someone who is passive-aggressive is emotionally wearing. Since they cannot react to a bad situation with the appropriate emotions and assertiveness themselves, they may narrate a story in which they have been used or exploited, but in a strangely disconnected manner. Suddenly, you are left 'doing the anger' for them. For instance, your passive-aggressive spouse may repeatedly tell you the story of how they are being bullied by their boss. However, they may narrate the story in an emotionally disconnected way, and never take any action to resolve the issue. You are left feeling rage on their behalf. In the end, you may seem more aggravated than they do. This is the quintessential way they discharge their anger. This child-like behaviour of dodging accountability can be likened to a child coming back from school and telling their mother that they've been bullied, expecting mum to do something on their behalf. While such a relationship dynamic may be appropriate in a parent-child relationship, it is problematic in what is supposed to be an equal adult-to-adult partnership.

Most of the time, the toxicity of the relationship dynamic with someone who is predominantly passive-aggressive is subtle and insidious. It can leave you with a sense of dissatisfaction, discomfort and intense irritation. The reason for these feelings may not be obvious to you, but passive-aggressiveness can rouse your anger just as much as an active display of hostility. The passive-aggressive person provokes other people's anger energies, but are not aware of their own part in the situation. A passive-aggressive person's hostility is usually masked with the guise of gentleness, niceness, innocence and patience. This facade may make you feel confused as to why such a kind and generous person could annoy you. Without careful attention and a particular kind of awareness, their dormant aggression is not noticeable. Therefore, it is particularly important to recognize when passive-aggressiveness becomes a form of covert abuse, especially when it is disguised in seemingly harmless, or even loving behaviours.

## WHAT IS GOING ON FOR THEM?

Most people who resort to using passive-aggressive behaviour do not consciously choose to do so. The way they react to or perceive things and events comes from a sense of internal insecurity and fear of confrontation. Sometimes without conscious awareness, they feel that they do not have the right to feel or to express their discontent. Deep inside they often feel inferior, or are afraid of the person they are angry with. They may be extremely frightened of having any friction or conflicts, and will avoid them at all costs. This means they would rather suppress their needs or shy away from issues in a relationship that need to be addressed.

Usually, a passive-aggressive way of dealing with the world is deeply ingrained, likely arising in a person's childhood and extending into adulthood. They may have learned it from their parents who were also passive-aggressive. Or it might have been the only choice they had when growing up in a hostile and unloving environment, where direct expressions of feelings were punished.

Many people who have developed passivity as a way of coping describe themselves as having a mild and tolerant temperament. They truly believe that they are patient and loving – which they probably are, but the problem is that they do not recognize their own shadow side.

Therefore, they are sincerely dismayed when confronted with their behaviour. Some passive-aggressive people constantly feel that the world is coming at them. Due to their lack of insight into their own personality, they say that others misunderstand them, or are holding them to unreasonable standards. They do not recognize that they have been irritating or subtly provocative in a situation.

Despite our frustrations in dealing with passive-aggressive people, it is important to remember that, most of the time, they do not do it maliciously or even consciously; they simply do not know any other way of dealing with their own pain. In the end, passive-aggressive behaviour is their survival strategy. It is a way of coping with their unmourned grief, unexpressed anger and the pain of unmet needs.

### WHAT DO I DO WITH SOMEONE WHO IS PASSIVE-AGGRESSIVE?

If you recognize that you are dealing with someone who is passive-aggressive, you can coach yourself to deal with the situation in a mature and assertive manner. For instance, you may say to yourself something along the following lines:

▶ 'I have a feeling this may be passive-aggressive behaviour.'

▶ 'I will not participate in this unproductive passive-aggressive conflict cycle.'

▶ 'It is their feelings of anger and resentment that they are unwilling to express to me openly.'

- ► 'I recognize that I feel angry too, but if I start reacting or act out of frustration, it will end up becoming my problem rather than theirs.'

- ► 'Instead, I take back control of my own feelings where I can.'

- ► 'Inside them is probably a fearful person who has never learned how to deal with their anger.'

- ► 'I am dealing with someone emotionally childish, so I ought to stay grounded in my adult position.'

- ► 'Perhaps when I am calmer, I can try and hold them in mind with compassion. However, that does not mean I compromise my boundaries.'

If possible, see if you can have an honest, assertive and productive discussion about the toxic nature of such behaviour. If the other party is not open to change, however, you may want to re-evaluate the relationship and negotiate the degree of closeness and distance you want to have. If this has been their life strategy since childhood, which is often the case, there may not be a quick and instant way of changing it. It takes conscious and continuous work, with patience and day-by-day commitment.

## Reflection prompts

The first and most important step is to recognize the signs of passive-aggressive behaviour on time, and to be mindful not to fall into the trap of unjustifiable shame and guilt. Look out for the obvious signs such as silent treatment or the use of withdrawal as a punishment. More importantly, look out for the subtle signs by listening to what your body and feelings say, especially when it comes to building a new relationship with someone.

Find a time and space to be with your journal. Sitting comfortably, bring your awareness to your breathing. Then ask yourself the following questions:

1 How do I feel after (not during) spending an extended period of time with this person?

2 When they say something, can I believe that they mean it, or do I feel like they don't mean what they say?

3 Do I feel confused, frustrated or irritated?

4 Do I feel able to be honest and open about my own needs?

5 Do I feel like I am relating to an emotionally robust and independent adult?

6 Am I currently, or have I ever been, in a relationship with someone who is passive-aggressive? (Evaluate relationships that you find draining in various parts of your life, including work relationships, friendships and intimate bonds, both in the past and in the present.)

7 How might my empathic nature be used to 'sponge up' their passive anger?

8 How do interactions with these people affect my physical, mental and emotional wellbeing?

In the end, it is not your job to take care of or to cure the dysfunctional emotional pattern of another person. You can only act productively if you take care of your own needs first. If you can stop blaming yourself for everything that happens in a relationship, or assuming that there is something wrong with you, you can listen to your inner guidance, and with understanding, compassion and assertiveness, turn your empathic ability into a strength.

# Seeing your shadow

So far, we have covered the impact of psychological projections and attacks, as well as passive-aggressive behaviour. However, the challenges we face when cohabiting with others in a psychological-energetic field are much more nuanced and complex, in which a 'me vs. them' approach is not helpful. The deeper reality is that sometimes, the very feeling that we have 'picked up' from others is likely pointing to something in us – whether we are aware of it or not. In other words, you are not experiencing something outside of yourself, but tapping into a collective consciousness that you are part of.

According to psychologist Carl Jung, in addition to our immediate consciousness, which is of a thoroughly personal nature, there exists another psychic realm that is collective, universal and impersonal. In recent years, through animal and human studies, scientists have verified the existence of a field of collective consciousness that is composed of all our individual consciousness. In particular, researchers in the areas of quantum physics and quantum psychology have found evidence that our collective consciousness is electromagnetic in nature (Grandpierre, 1996), and that we are indeed all interrelated at the level of cells and tissue (Adamski, 2011). When you become resentful for picking up other people's 'negative energies', or if you begin to see their negative traits as a threat to your wellbeing, you have not recognized this one facet of the truth: there isn't a real separation between you and others.

Sometimes, we have strong reactions to people that, on the surface, make no logical sense. It can be any person, from a colleague to a random stranger, even when in reality we do not know much about them. When this happens, you may find yourself acting in ways that are out-of-character, or experience strong anger, disgust and aversion that do not seem justifiable.

Carl Jung's idea of the Shadow helps us understand what is going on (1946). Jung proposed that in most of our daily lives we live with a known 'Persona'. Our Persona is made up of a notion of ourselves that we recognize, acknowledge and attach to; these are often influenced by what society and our upbringing have taught us. The Persona involves labels and descriptions that we are comfortable with: 'I am a loving mother', 'I am a good citizen, and I obey the law', 'I am a caring person, and I genuinely want my friends to be happy'. These descriptions are real aspects of ourselves, but not the full picture.

On the other side of our Persona is our Shadow, which consists of the parts of ourselves that we reject and disown. Since we do not like to think of these aspects, we keep them dormant and untouched in the unconscious, until the day they get unexpectedly triggered by people and events. It is in those times that you find yourself acting out in ways that surprise or even frighten you.

What happens is that we tend to project our Shadow onto other people. When we feel the need to shut down against an 'other', it is because what is in front of us triggers unfamiliar and unpleasant feelings. On a deeper level, we resent them for bringing forth aspects of ourselves that we do not want to acknowledge or recognize. Therefore, when you find yourself feeling irrationally irritated or disgusted by aspects of someone's behaviour, it can point to something you are frightened of seeing or having in yourself. When suppressed or projected, your Shadow can become destructive; it may erupt in depression, aggression towards yourself or hostility towards others.

Knowing and owning your Shadow is challenging at first, but it can be an extremely fruitful and illuminating experience. Although we do not realize it, it takes a lot of energy to push down parts of ourselves. Holistic health and true self-esteem are achieved when we can take in all dimensions of ourselves, including our propensities to be angry, self-preserving, needy and envious. Ultimately, learning to accept the fullness of who you are, both good and bad, light and dark, is both the first and the final step towards psychological integration.

### Exercise: hugging my shadow

How do you know when some 'shadow work' is warranted? When you find yourself wanting to put a block between yourself and others, or becoming disturbingly judgemental, you can pause and reflect on the possibility of a Shadow trigger being in operation.

Working with your Shadow is challenging because the purpose of the Shadow is to protect you from enacting personal characteristics that, if expressed, might give you a sense of unease – after all, that is why you have stuffed these aspects of yourself in the corner of your psyche in the first place. Therefore, follow this process carefully, and have self-compassion running in the background at all times.

Find a place that is quiet and private, and use your journal for the following reflections:

1   Identify a person from your life who triggers strong, unpleasant feelings in you. They can be distant or close, but ideally not a family member.

Choose someone to whom you tend to overreact emotionally; their behaviour may disturb you, or their traits cause disgust and aversion in you. This person can be from the past or present, as long as you notice sufficient emotional charge when you think of them.

2   Identify three to five traits or characteristics in this person that particularly disturb you, or trigger strong feelings in you.

3   Now, see if you can be open to the idea that these may be some of your disowned parts. Look for versions of these traits in yourself, perhaps in subtle or unexpressed ways. Repeat the following sentences by filling in the blanks with the identified attributes:

   ✳ 'I am open to the idea that I have the potential to be ..., too.'
   ✳ 'I am open to the thought that I can be ..., too, even if only occasionally, and in certain circumstances.'

4   Challenge yourself to come up with three ways in which you exhibit some of these traits or characteristics. Remember, even if you do possess these traits, they are only part of you, not the whole of you. They do not have to be prominent features of your personality.

5   Describe the emotions (anger, fear, sadness, jealousy, envy, guilt, grief, shame) that owning these traits have evoked in you.

6   End the exercise by repeating the following message (either by writing it down, or speaking it out loud): 'Even when this is difficult to digest or accept, even when what comes up is at odds with who I think I am, I fully love and accept who I am.'

# Embracing your light

In the last section, we looked at the concept of the Shadow, and what happens when we share an energetic and psychological field with other people.

In truth, we project not only our unwanted traits, but also our light and virtues onto others. In the same way your suppressed Shadow triggers you, if you find yourself immensely attracted to certain people, that is pointing to your aspirations, as well as the positive attributes and qualities that you have yet to recognize in yourself.

This is a useful concept to grasp, as it provides valuable information for your self-actualization. To reach your full potential, you ought to first identify a sense of purpose that is unique to you. Often, this is not immediately clear, and you may summon the help of teachers, mentors, and role models. A wisdom seeker is one who proactively learns from whomever or whatever is presented to them on any given day. As a Chinese saying goes: 'Of every three people you meet, one of them is your teacher.' Historically, seeking a master formed an essential part of any journey towards growth and enlightenment. Fortunately for us, today we live in a truly global community where at our fingertips are knowledge and wisdom from all around the world. We no longer have to find our masters by going on a long pilgrimage, and our learning is no longer bound to geographical locations. Instead of having only one master, we can use the internet to seek out our teachers from anywhere in the world, across all media. Your virtual mentors may be people who have achieved success in your chosen field, or those who have created work that inspires you. Perhaps you find yourself nodding along with what they say, or that you have a similar vision to what they have achieved. If you look deeper, you will realize that the people you are attracted to serve as the portal for you to rediscover your gifts, your interests, your skills, the 'sandbox' you want to play in, and the corner of the world you wish to occupy. Maybe you start by observing the way they compose themselves, the way they act and speak, and the way they interact with the world and people around them. However, what you ultimately want to find, and ought to find, is a set of beliefs, values, and a model for psycho-spiritual progression that mirrors your own. All that any teacher or model can do, is to help you to unlock the wisdom that is already in you. No one can actually give you anything you don't already possess. They may point the way, but ultimately what you seek is inside of you.

Being aware of the virtues that you are not actively manifesting is an essential step in finding your legacy. Through reviewing the words, images, events and individuals that have an impact on you, you begin to get in touch with your aspirations. It is through a constant process of collecting and studying external materials that you gradually find the way to your own legacy.

# Exercise: reclaiming your light

Use your journal for the following exercise.

1   Think about the characters or role models that have a substantial and direct impact on you, or identify the people for whom you feel great admiration or affection.

2   In your journal, list the qualities or virtues that you are drawn to. Examples of this may include integrity, honesty, kindness, patience or wisdom.

3   Write these virtues down in your journal. Then next to each one, reflect on and write down times in your life when you have exhibited these qualities. Take some time to acknowledge the fact that, even though dormant, these qualities are in you too.

4   Whether or not you struggle with step 3, try to reflect on the following questions: What might have caused you to suppress these aspects of yourself? Were they criticized, shunned or denied at some stage in your life? Was the fear of power in operation?

5   Consider how you might change if you were to embrace these previously disowned qualities. What are some of the ways in which you could integrate these qualities into your current way of being? How could you use them to benefit you?

6   Finally, ask yourself: If I were to fully manifest these qualities or virtues that matter to me, where would I be? What would I be doing? Who would I be surrounded by?

7   If you can visualize it, come up with a vivid image, and write down or draw what you see.

# Finding true intimacy

# Knowing when the past is present

Because of the intensity of their expressions, many emotionally intense people are accused of being the 'emotionally unstable', 'immature' or 'dramatic' ones in relationships. More often than not, however, their reactions are not signs of a disorder, but amplified versions of reactions we have to unhealed wounds inflicted in the past.

You may find that you have certain 'buttons' that, when pushed, cause you to react or behave in uncontrollable ways. Or, you find yourself running into the same kind of relationship problems with particular types of people. A concept in psychology, called transference, may help us understand these relationship phenomena. The more we know about how our mind works when it comes to relating to other people, the more resourceful we can be in understanding and managing our emotional intensity.

Transference is when we unconsciously project an old relationship onto a current one. The concept is Freudian, but it does not only happen in the therapist's chair. We can think of transference as a form of displacement. Sometimes in our day-to-day life, we catch ourselves displacing our feelings towards A onto B. For example, I may be angry with my boss, but I take it out on my partner. In transference, we displace the feelings we have towards people from our past, like our parents or ex-partners, on to those in the here and now. To 'transfer' means we carry what is in the past into the present, and most of the time it happens without our being consciously aware of it. A common saying that captures the essence of transference is: 'You are treating me as if I were your mother'. Transference can come up anywhere, in any relationship – from friendships and intimate relationships, to strangers. Usually, our closest relationship triggers the most fear and projection; this is why friendships always seem much easier to manage than romantic partnerships.

When a new person enters our life, we are most vulnerable to experiencing both powerful positive and negative transference. We both idealize and demonize our partner: we are in love, but we also find ourselves getting triggered into intense anger and frustration. We fantasize the best and assume the worst. We may project a fairytale onto the relationship, but when conflicts happen, or when our sensitivities are triggered, our new partner suddenly becomes our worst enemy.

Positive transference explains the intense attraction or infatuation we feel at the beginning of romance. When we first meet someone, despite having limited factual information, we tend to 'fill in the gaps' with things that we have been fantasizing about. We may exaggerate or diminish traits we see in another. One tendency is to unconsciously create in our mind an idealized version of our new partner, just like the prince and princess we have always dreamed of, and project our vision onto the current reality. For example, if my father had been cold, ignorant and neglectful, I may exaggerate the moments when my new partner shows signs of being attentive, insightful and loving, and believe that he is 'the one'. While this process is natural and not 'wrong', it can lead to disappointment. Sometimes, the deprived child inside us has the compulsion to fill the void with a child-like mentality, which drives us to demand immediate and unconditional love as a baby would with their caregiver. Unrealistic positive transference almost always leads to disillusionment, for even the healthiest adult relationship cannot realistically fulfil our cravings for the 'perfect love'. As a result, we might cycle in and out of infatuation. One minute, we believe that we have found The One, and in the next minute we have our hopes and fantasies shattered by disappointment.

The opposite can also happen. In the case of negative transference, we are triggered by qualities and events that remind us of our deepest wounds and of what was missing in our childhood. Sudden, intense and inexplicable rage is a telling sign of transference. For instance, if a boy had grown up being constantly criticized and controlled by his overpowering mother, he may have become extremely sensitive to others invading his space or depriving him of his freedom. His sensitivity manifests itself in the present day in the form of extreme reactivity. When he feels stressed at work, and his wife calls him, the strong feeling of being intruded upon and controlled is invoked. He finds himself getting into a rage and blaming his wife for not giving him enough space. All of this may be unconscious: looking back, he wonders why he reacted aggressively when, logically, he knew that his wife was not his mother, and was not trying to control him. When negative transference is at play, we are not reacting from our adult, rational mind, but from our emotional sore spots. These strong feelings may seem 'out of proportion' when we look at the present event but are entirely appropriate when seen in the context of a hurting child.

Having a need for attention, affection, appreciation and acknowledgement is not pathological. It is when we are starved of love that our needs turn into a hungry, all-encompassing beast. Deprived, we become wounded children with adult exteriors, desperate for unconditional positive regard, attention around-the-clock and endless affection. Of course, there is nothing wrong with two adults meeting each other's emotional needs in a relationship, but such intense cravings for love may be unrealistic for adult-to-adult encounters. Ultimately, we will struggle to find lasting fulfilment from the outside world if we are not able to give it to ourselves.

Transference has the potential to be destructive, but it is also a doorway to growth and insight. When we acknowledge a transference, we also cease to blame our current partner for our feelings and instead begin to find what we had needed. When the unconscious is made conscious, our transference provides crucial information about our inner world and our original wounds, and opens up a door to profound healing and integration.

**TIPS AND STRATEGIES: WORKING WITH NEGATIVE TRANSFERENCE**
Negative transference has the potential to produce destructive hatred, and it mostly stems from disappointments in early life. When we are in the web of transference, we cannot see reality clearly. Unconscious transference holds us back from intimacy, from our best self and from emotional freedom. Becoming aware of transference opens the door to much more presence and joy in our lives.

To break free from negative transference, we start by noticing it, and then working through it with kindness and gentleness. When you can make your transference conscious and recognize it in yourself, you will no longer be bound in endless loops of reactivity. Here are some steps that may help you in the process.

### ▶ 1 Refraining from reactivity

How do you know you are having a 'transference reaction'? It's not always obvious, but you probably are if you find yourself having a strong response that seems unjustifiable based on its apparent triggers.

Think about certain people that set off your intense reactions. Before you launch into an emotional outburst, you can be prepared for your triggers. The goal here is to catch the impulse that precedes your reactivity, so you do not end up in unproductive behaviour and destructive actions towards yourself or others. In the heat of the moment, you may use one or more of the following strategies:

▶ Exit the immediate situation until your high emotions subside or resolve. If you are caught in an intense conflict with another person, don't be afraid to take a timeout and resume communication later. If you feel anger surging up, avoid all destructive or passive-aggressive behaviour such as rolling your eyes and finger pointing.

▶ Stay connected with the sensations in your body – become aware of your heartbeat, breathing, and any tightening of your body parts such as clenching your jaw or your fists. The feeling you get when you are caught up in transference is similar to the emotional experience of fear: even when there is no immediate threat, your body remains on guard, and your mind becomes fixated on what might go wrong. Remind yourself that no matter what happens, you are safe.

▶ Breathe, and you may find counting back from ten to zero helpful. As you inhale, inhale fully and imagine cool air going all the way through your lungs into your abdomen. As you exhale, exhale fully and imagine emptying yourself of some of the tension.

► Stop yourself from any actions that come from reactive or self-destructive impulses, even if this means distracting yourself temporarily. Choose activities that you find pleasurable and soothing from taking a hot bath/shower, or going for a walk, to listening to calm music – anything that is quickly accessible and works for you. The point here is not to avoid dealing with your feelings, but to buy yourself some time, so you can make some mental space to enable you to move on to the next step.

### ► 2 Noticing your experience non-judgementally

Once you have created some mental space between the stimulus and your reactions, you can practise the skills of identifying and putting words to your experience non-judgementally. One way is to develop the part of you that can observe your thoughts and feelings without getting caught up in them.

Take a step back, and ask yourself the following questions – work through them one by one, slowly and gently. As best you can, stay open and curious, rather than self-critical.

► 'What am I feeling right now?'

► 'If this feeling is familiar, what or whom does it remind me of?'

► 'Has something sad or troubling from the past been brought back up by the immediate trigger?'

► 'Have I felt this sadness before?'

► 'When was the first time I experienced this?'

► 'Is there an underlying, lingering feeling that has always been with me, in the background?'

### ► 3 Working with what comes up

Perhaps nothing comes up. Sometimes your current emotional reaction has nothing to do with your past. It may be that you are simply humiliated and angry. But if indeed you are reminded of an old relationship, this is an excellent opportunity to clear up some old blockages that you carry. Sometimes this involves deeper grief work. Because transference is mostly driven by our unmet needs, in the process of uncovering its roots, we may find old wounds and trauma. In this process, you may need to summon the most resilient and mature part of your adult self to defend, or to sooth the part inside of you that feels young and vulnerable. Since transference creates an 'emotional time warp' that transfers your emotional past and psychological needs into the present, being honest with yourself about the core issues behind your immediate triggers is essential. Reflect on the following questions:

▶ 'Who did I have the old relationship with?'

▶ 'What was the nature of that relationship?'

▶ 'What were the relationship dynamics? Was I locked in a fixed role?'

▶ 'What wasn't I able to do – probably because I was too young or vulnerable – that I wish I could have done?'

▶ 'If I was to go back in time and stand up for myself, what would I do differently?'

▶ 'What might I say or do to the person who originally hurt me?'

### ▶ 4 Appreciating the present reality

Now, go back to the person who triggers you in the present, and see if anything feels different.

When we can break through the trance of transference, we will be able to relate to each other as who we truly are, without the clouded judgement, without bringing the past into the present, and without the stories and mental chatters that have burdened us. Real intimacy happens when two people relate to each other in an authentic way. In this form of real relationship, we are present. We appreciate each other with no hidden agenda or anticipation. We go into it with real presence and participation. A couple engaged in this dimension are two people going on an exciting journey together, curious about each other, looking forward to finding out the unknown. With enough practice, we can find the courage to enter the here-and-now reality of ourselves and others, and not be haunted by shadows from the past. Only then we are open to the real intimacy, joy and beauty right in front of us.

## Saying 'no' to bad relationships

Have you ever found yourself repeating the same destructive relationship pattern? Or, do you find yourself getting drawn to unsuitable, emotionally unavailable, rejecting, or even exploitative partners, and overstaying in these relationships?

All human beings have a need to be seen, heard, attended to, and accepted and loved for who they are. For those of us who did not receive the care we needed as children, however, these unmet needs do not just disappear. They remain within us, often in distorted forms, growing ever more insatiable. If we are not aware of our compelling yearnings and able to find adequate ways of taking care of them, we may end up with repeated relationship problems.

The developmental differences of emotionally intense and gifted people can be alienating. From a young age, you sensed that the way you experienced the world was fundamentally different from your peers and your parents. In the social world, you may find that others frequently misunderstand your vocabulary and humour, and you struggle to fit into any social groups. For the gifted, social alienation is not a result of mental disturbance, but the lack of suitable peer groups.

From as early as a pre-verbal age, you have felt an omnipresent sense of feeling like a Martian visiting the Earth. The painful reminders of being the misunderstood and invisible child can persist into adulthood: apathetic reactions, blank stares, misunderstandings, all serve as reminders of how painful it was to be the 'missed' sensitive child.

Moreover, your advanced development may also have made it difficult to find many adults or authority figures to trust and depend upon fully. Maybe you had to shoulder adult responsibilities at a young age or had been forced into providing emotional support for dependent friends, family members and your parents. Thus, deep down, you may always be looking for that one person you can lean on, comfortably and assuredly. As a result, at the beginning of a budding romance, for instance, you may become overly hopeful and craft a glorified – and ultimately false – picture of the other person, so long as they show any sign of potentially satiating your unmet needs. You may ignore any warning signs that suggest otherwise. In other cases, you may sacrifice other needs in your life for a temporary sense of a shared emotional reality.

Your compelling feelings are not in themselves harmful. They are innocent longings that come from a younger part of yourself. As both an adult and a child, you have fundamental needs to be seen and heard, to have role models that you can emulate and learn from, and for a sense of belonging with people who share at least some resemblance to you.

When you find someone who can listen with the empathy and attentiveness that you have long craved, your old unmet needs will be awakened. Some part of you is convinced that your partner is someone who can, at last, meet your needs.

Your tendency to be attracted to a particular type of individual, or get into certain kinds of relationship dynamics, may essentially be a compulsion to return to your past to remove old blockages. Behind your repetition of expectation is the hope for something new and healing. If the original relationship was unhealthy or lacking, you may be trying to gain closure. The old, wounded relationship is unfinished in the sense that there are some things we didn't have the capacity to do at the time with the original characters, leaving behind certain unmet needs and deep longings. Sometimes, you can no longer work out the issues with the original characters such as your parents. They might have passed away, or continue to deny or invalidate your truth, or they may simply lack the mental capacity to work things through with you. In your innate ability to search for wholeness, you will seek in your current life someone with whom you can enter into a new relationship that has dynamics similar to the old one. By replaying the old narratives, you replicate the unfinished business in the hope that you can 'get it right' this time. Even if your conscious mind says you never want to end up in the same situation, your unconscious drive is to keep trying until it can rewrite the ending. As a result, you may find yourself stuck in repetitive loops with unfulfilling relationships or exploitative partners.

## FORMS OF COMPROMISED RELATIONSHIP

### ▶ Exploitative relationships

Exploitation involves a regular pattern of verbal offence, threatening, bullying and constant criticism, as well as more subtle tactics like intimidation, shaming and manipulation. Emotional boundary violation happens when one party uses mental tactics to gain power and control in a relationship, and this often occurs because they have been abused themselves.

It is not always easy to tell if you are in an emotionally exploitative relationship, as some forms are more easily recognized than others. You may be emotionally violated and psychologically abused without realizing it: passive-aggressive behaviour, for instance, is often subtle and insidious.

Your tendency to be self-critical and highly reflective can lead you to blame yourself rather than others, and you may make excuses for others' exploitative behaviour. If you suffer from low self-esteem, you may feel you have to 'take what you can get', and tolerate a dissatisfying or exploitative relationship. By not valuing yourself, you remain with a partner who does not provide you with the right kind of nourishment.

If as a child your empathic gifts were exploited, you might subconsciously recreate situations or relationships where the pattern is similar. We are naturally drawn to, and attract to us, the people who treat us in ways that feel familiar. As long as you are reacting unconsciously to your childhood emotional wounds and compulsion, you may just keep repeating the same patterns.

Here are some questions that may help you to reflect on whether or not you are in an exploitative relationship:

1  Do they accuse me of being 'too sensitive', especially when I react to their abusive comments?

2  Do they belittle or humiliate me in subtle or obvious ways?

3   Do they regularly dismiss my opinions, viewpoints and suggestions?

4   Do they sometimes use sarcasm or 'teasing' as a way to put me down?

5   Do they respect my 'no' or do they repeatedly cross my boundaries?

6   Do they blame their unhappiness on me?

7   Do they call me names?

8   Do they use emotional distancing or withdrawal as a way to punish me?

9   Do they make me feel that the abuse is my fault and that they would not have to act that way if I did x, y, or z?

## ▶ Unbalanced relationship

Another form of compromised relationship is an unbalanced one. All relationships have some difficulties, but big differences in the levels of emotional development between the couple can create an especially challenging dynamic to the point where it is unhealthy. If you've ever felt as if you are becoming the other person's confidante, counsellor, or even caregiver, then it is likely that you are in an unbalanced relationship.

It is easy to fall into this role: after all, sensitive people are natural emotional carers. Those with increased perceptivity and empathy will notice the subtle body language and behavioural signals that are missed by most. You may automatically slip into the role of helping others feel comfortable and soothed, either through physical actions or with consolations and close listening. If you've carried the role of being the one everyone goes to in your family, the caregiver role might have become your second nature.

In an unbalanced relationship, your partner may not intend to exploit you, but the relationship is by default imbalanced due to the discrepancy in your sensory receptivities and processing capacities. Your maturity may allow you to offer compassion or the listening ear that they need, but they may not be able to do the same for you. Or you may become overwhelmed by insights or clues into the relationship dynamic which your partner cannot see, feel or share. You can read their mind, but they cannot read yours; thus, you may have to reflect on behalf of both yourself and your partner, always explain yourself, or become wrapped up in 'educating' your partner on your needs.

One-sided relationships such as these can subject you to undue stress. As equal footing in the relationship is lost, so too is deep intimacy. You may begin to feel overwhelmed by your fixed role. Ultimately, being the caregiver for of your partner is actually of little benefit to them: for they, like you, must eventually find their solace within.

Here are some questions that may help you to reflect on whether or not you are in an unbalanced relationship:

1   Am I giving support to my partner at the cost of my physical, psychological and spiritual wellbeing?

2   Do I sometimes feel resentful for the skewed give/take balance in this relationship?

3   Do I have a strong desire for more freedom and independence, but feel guilty when I do not take care of the other person?

4   Do I remain silent to avoid conflicts, or to protect my partner's feelings?

5   Do I struggle to find someone who I am both romantically attracted to and find intellectually stimulating?

6   Do I consistently feel frustrated and impatient with my partner because they are unable to keep up with me?

7   Do I regularly feel that I am 'too much' (emotionally, intellectually, physically) for them?

8   Do I sometimes feel more like a carer, teacher or mentor to my partner, rather than an equal?

# Exercise: relationship patterns

Use the questions to examine whether you have a tendency to be locked in unhealthy relationship patterns. Reflect on your existing relationship, and try to be a fair witness to what is going on. If you find yourself being locked in an exploitative or unbalanced relationship, the most important first step is to relinquish any self-blame. Your drive to be in these relationships is simply an indication that there are certain unmet needs, and the root of your yearnings is always pure and should be treated with interest and respect. Ultimately, the step to freedom is to stop seeking womb-like, all-encompassing, unconditional adoration from others. If you can give up the compulsion to demand from others what you didn't get or can't give to yourself, then you are truly free.

1 What do I want from a relationship?

2 What are some of my personal boundaries?

3 Where in my life can I practise assertiveness skills, and to ask directly for what I want?

4 Do I have a 'bottom line'? If so, what is it? What limits do I set on the number of times I will allow someone to disappoint me or invade my boundaries before I decide to move on?

5 What are my needs? How are they being met and not met in my current relationship?

6 In what ways can I develop the ability to be my own best friend, best listener and even best lover?

7 Can I get my emotional needs met from multiple sources, rather than by one single person?

8 How can I channel my desire to be seen and heard into my vocation or a creative pursuit?

# Avoiding burnout and bore-out

For any of us to function as happy, integrated human beings, we must continually work towards achieving an optimal level of arousal, where we are not over- or under-stimulated by our physical environment and mental input. This is also where we enter into our most grounded, resourceful and creative state. Because of your intensity, however, what you need might differ from what conventional wisdom suggests.

Contemporary thinking around dealing with introversion or high sensitivity tends to focus on the risk of over-arousal. In *The Highly Sensitive Person in Love* (2001), for instance, Dr Elaine Aron speaks extensively about the problems of a highly sensitive person (HSP) becoming overwhelmed with stimulation when they get together with a non-HSP. Yet the other side of the picture – the risk of being under-aroused in a relationship, has not been explored. Over-committing to social activities may not satisfy your rich inner life, as many conventional activities such as going to parties or to the cinema may not be what you are interested in. On the other hand, frantically avoiding activities because you are 'too sensitive' can be just as problematic. For the emotionally intense and gifted, it isn't that you need to avoid all stimulants, but you need to find the right kind of contact and in the right doses.

When you enter into an intimate relationship with another person where there is a huge discrepancy in your level of intensity, a myriad of problems can arise. You may find that you have to hide your true self due to the gap in your levels of sensory receptivity and processing capacity. You may have to consciously slow down your speech and your thoughts, bury your intense feelings, hold back your excitement, dilute complex ideas and concepts, or withhold your seemingly 'out-of-proportion' (based on what society considers 'normal') passion about certain topics. Or perhaps, without knowing quite why, you find yourself feeling bored, restless and irritated over minor things. If you and your partner do not share the same depth of passion, you may feel more lonely in a relationship than when you are single. You may wish to be alone – or even fantasize about time all to yourself – while you are with your partner. Your sex drive may plummet, and you may feel guilty for lacking desire for your partner. In some cases, you may even subconsciously try to 'shrink' or censor yourself to protect your partner's feelings, especially if you have been conditioned, either by society's standards or your own upbringing, to take care of others' emotional needs before your own. In the long run, even with strong physical or emotional attraction, such a relationship will become dissatisfying and stressful for both parties.

## HAVE YOU SUFFERED FROM BURNOUT OR BORE-OUT IN YOUR RELATIONSHIP?

### ▶ Burnout

Burnout can happen when a sensitive person enters into an intimate relationship with someone with a different temperament. It happens when you don't honour your need for solitude, reflection, agency and autonomy, or when you stretch beyond your limits to comply with society's standards of how you should behave. It is also caused by being unable to say 'no' to activities that deplete you.

As a result of being over-stimulated, you may experience signs of chronic stress reactions due to an overload of the sympathetic nervous system. Mentally, this may show up as chronic anxiety, or a lingering sense of depression. Common physical symptoms are adrenal fatigue, thyroid problems, digestive issues, chronic pain, shortness of breath, and insomnia. You may also experience ailments that cannot be medically explained, such as allergies, chronic fatigue and irritable bowel syndrome. In addition, your environmental sensitivities might be heightened, making loud noises, strong odours, etc. unbearable. As a result, you may find yourself resorting to excessive self-soothing behaviours, such as comfort eating or over-spending.

### ▶ Bore-out

Bore-out tends to happen when an intense and gifted person enters a relationship with someone who does not match their level of emotional, intellectual or spiritual intensity. Here are some of the signs:

▶ You feel restless, irritated, impatient and intolerant of your partner.

▶ You find yourself 'nit-picking' your partner's negative qualities.

- ▶ You feel empty and bored when you are with your spouse.

- ▶ You miss your own time and space and even fantasize about being on your own again.

- ▶ You feel more emotionally lonely when you are with your partner than when you are on your own.

- ▶ You feel a lack of sex drive and passion (which may also spill over into your life as a general feeling of lethargy and boredom).

- ▶ You feel like a 'bad person' for being irritable and unloving.

## WHAT IF YOUR CURRENT PARTNER DOES NOT MEET YOUR NEEDS?

When it comes to a romantic or intimate relationship, it is often difficult for the emotionally intense to find another person who can match their depth of feelings, rigour in their insights, or the complexity of their thinking. For many reasons, you may choose to stay with someone with a different temperament or level of emotional intensity.

This does not mean you have to go down the path of despair or constant disappointment. In fact, it is unrealistic to expect one person to fulfil all your physical, psychological and spiritual needs. If your intimate partner does not meet all your needs, you can be honest about the reality of your situation and move on to proactively find a way to meet your needs via other means, such as with close friends, community, therapy or connection with your spiritual source.

## SEEKING OUT NOURISHING INTERACTION

To have a fulfilling life, it is important that you know how to find interactions that are adequately stimulating and fulfilling for you, both within and outside of your romantic companionship.

When you are with someone who matches your level of intensity intellectually, emotionally and even spiritually, you can easily enter into the 'flow' state – that is, a state of optimal experience (see Chapter 10). As conceptualized by Csíkszentmihályi, people are at their happiest, most productive and most creative when in such state, where there is immense joy and deep fulfilment.

strategies to keep yourself safe, such as keeping everyone at bay so that you won't get hurt. The part of you that feels grief-stricken may begin to persuade you to stop caring. It will likely urge you to be 'less attached' to people and things. Your senses may be dulled, erasing the beauty around you. Eventually, your world becomes less colourful and vivid, less full of life and love. You may feel that you are protecting yourself from heartbreaks, yet end up living half-heartedly.

## PROTEST, DESPAIR, DETACHMENT

Those of us who lacked a secure attachment to an early caregiver are more likely to overuse detachment as a coping strategy. In their seminal work on attachment, psychologists Bowlby and Robertson looked at what happens to children when they experience traumatic separation and loss (Bowlby *et al.*, 1952). The scholars discerned three separate stages that typically occur to children when traumatically separated from their caregivers: Protest, Despair and Detachment. Imagine pulling a young child away from their mother. At first, they cry profusely and look around for her. This is the Protest phase. If the mother manages to come and retrieve the child in time, then the distress is alleviated. However, if the mother's absence continues, the child will then enter the stage of Despair: becoming quiet, withdrawn and apathetic, having given up on the hope that their mother will return. As this goes on, they will enter the Detachment phase, where the need for anyone is relinquished. Even if the mother returns, the child will appear to hardly know her – and no longer feel any attachment to her. Their relationship with their mother and the world has become shallow and untrusting. This is a difficult stage ever to exit once entered.

In other words, if your early caregivers had been emotionally unstable or unavailable, your memories might have taught you that there is 'no point' in being needy and that it is safer not to be dependent on anyone. When a relationship begins to become close, you may fear the potential attachment. Or you may become extremely self-sufficient, exulting in a temporary sense of comfort and control. Perhaps you swear never to fall in love to avoid disappointment, to push people away before they do the same to you, or even to pretend being in love while locking your heart away. In your wariness to trust, you may become unable to receive love and affection; even when others express genuine love and appreciation for you, your automatic response may be to dismiss them as not genuine or not 'real'. You may also turn to substitutes such as food and other compulsive, self-soothing behaviours to gratify your need for intimacy. While on the surface these distancing strategies have kept you 'safe', they come at a huge cost. As Gabrielle Bernstein (2011) poignantly put it: 'We sense love, but we don't believe in it. We save our faith for fear. But ultimately, there is a quiet voice in each of us that longs for something better.' When your emotional numbness turns into feeling empty, disconnected and lonely, you will realize that your protective shield has outlived its usefulness and is now keeping you from the life you want.

## DISMANTLING YOUR ARMOUR

This may seem counter-intuitive at first, but the ability to love arises from our ability to grieve for changes in life. The ever-changing nature of all things in this world means that to live wholeheartedly we must be accepting of losses and endings. Change is not only a fact of life, change *is* life. When we think about it, with each current moment there is the death of the last, with each today comes the passing away of yesterday. This applies to each and every single moment you spend with your loved ones; knowing that things will end and change makes us feel such tenderness and vulnerability whenever we open our hearts to love. This points to a poignant and beautiful fragility that is embedded in the very essence of being human.

Finding your way back into relatedness involves embracing the full spectrum of human experience. Since life does not come with guarantees, being alive also means some degree of vulnerability. Much like life, relationships are multiple and various, encompassing pain as well as pleasure, labour as well as play. In her seminal work on vulnerability, Brene Brown taught us that when we lose our tolerance for vulnerability, joy becomes foreboding (Brown, 2012). If we wish to circumvent everyday grief, we will eventually pay a high price. In our attempt to hide, we become cut off, numb and unable to feel joy; in our attempt to avoid pain, we sacrifice the capacity for joy and beauty. Therefore, to authentically engage with life means to wake up from a dream-like state, to acknowledge the impermanent nature of all things, and to embrace the ebb and flow of all that is in human life.

You are bound to feel vulnerable because, when you choose to live and open to others wholeheartedly, you now have a stake in the game. But your goal is not to avoid heartbreaks entirely, but to believe that you can survive them. Hurts and heartbreaks may happen but will also pass; your resilience is your secure base (see Chapter 9). No matter what happens, something within you will remain unchanged and unperturbed. It is by cultivating the courage to accept impermanence, losses and death that you can live life to the full. After all, as an emotionally gifted person, it is your ability to develop deep and meaningful relationships, to dive into sadness, to ponder death and parting, and to embrace existential angst, that marks your vitality.

## Exercise: working with your protector

### 1 Seeing behind your protector

Let's assume that there is a part of you, let's call it your 'protector', that likes to keep a safe distance from your intensities, especially if the feelings that come up when you are in a group or with another person. 'He' (it can be a he, she or it, whatever resonates best with you) has been there for a long time to help you cope with any overwhelming feelings that come your way. He must have been very useful and have played a very important role in your life.

However, it is time to retrieve the one who is behind the protector. In the process of dulling your pain, you have also dulled your joy, passion, tenderness, and even feelings of love. These feelings are still there but have been dampened. They are hiding right behind what may be 'calm' but also numb and flat.

It can feel very tender and vulnerable as the more innately passionate and innocent part of you finds their voice again. As your feelings and yearnings for connection come surging back, you may feel extra emotional. This is because, when you reunite with your inner buoyancy, you also get in touch with that you have disowned and rejected all these years. You may even find that you deeply miss your inner child or your teenage self. Coming to terms with what you have missed, you may experience a wave of complex feelings that involve guilt, sadness, fear and excitement. It is very natural and though you are not used to it, I can assure you that these feelings are safe.

## 2  Honouring your defences
There is no need to bury your protector altogether, for there is value in being maturely cautious in adult relationships. A child's innocence and limitless ability to trust is joyous yet incredibly vulnerable. And actually, the protector brings valuable, accumulated knowledge and experiences that make up your intuition. Your highly attuned intuitive skills allow you to very rapidly assess, through picking up the body language of others, the level of your safety. When skilfully honed, your protective intuition is a great protector. It is only when it becomes overly rigid and extreme that it makes life an exhausting battle against fear.

## 3  Soothing your protector
Remind your fearful protector that the highest purpose in life is not just to survive. You can educate him in the fact that life is by nature ever-changing, and the only way through is to adapt and flow. Tell him that it is silly to never let in joy for fear of losing it – that is as silly as never taking in nutritious food for fear of getting hungry again.

You may assure him that the worst part is already in the past, and you are now strong enough to gradually invite back the parts of you that feel tender, soft and emotional.

## 4  Remind yourself of how incredibly adaptable you are
You have been through bad things and have achieved great things. You have been doing this all your life, and all you need to do now is to reconnect with the strength that is inside you. The joy of whole-hearted relatedness and connection is only on the other side of the fence.

# Finding your way back into love
If you have been wounded in relationships before, and have used distancing as a defensive strategy, the process of coming out of your shell can be a challenging one. However, since your original pain finds its root in the relational world, it cannot be fully healed without allowing yourself to be vulnerable to another.

The existential tension between isolation and relatedness, and the desire to preserve oneself safely while being with others, are universal concerns shared, to some degree, by all of the humanity. As Eric Fromm (1956) proposed, a solution to this tension is 'relatedness'– the synthesis of closeness and uniqueness.

However frightening, the process of thawing your heart and letting in others is a worthwhile endeavour. When you can finally loosen your grip on the rigid wall that has kept you away from not just pain but also joy and connection, you will reach a new layer of tenderness within yourself. This is the purest, most natural part of you; your openheartedness is your natural state and has been with you all along. No matter how much you have tried to deny or bury it, your innocent self's yearning is always there, wanting to love and trust wholeheartedly, to immerse fully in love, and to experience exuberant joy and excitement.

The goal, however, is not to jump into the world with optimistic ignorance, unaware of social dynamics and danger, but to reach a point where you are not held back by old fears and unnecessary hyper-vigilance. Eventually, you learn to balance open-heartedness with feeling safe in the world.

As you enter the chasm of change, you are bound to feel a little wobbly. Your brain may perceive the feelings you get from opening up and trusting others as threats, and your mind believes that letting go will cause dangers and harm. A part of you is anxious about losses, betrayal and abandonment happening again. These are natural responses to change and uncertainty.

But you are not the only one who faces these challenges. When you open yourself inwardly to your relational vulnerabilities, you will also start to see a similar fear in those around you. For example, you may notice how an intimate partner or a dear friend distances themselves just as your connection begins to deepen. For many others who were not able to count on their early caregivers, their experience had led them to assume that you will also disappoint or betray them in the end. When you see the parallels in your journeys, there is the potential for you to enter a process of growing together.

Previously, you might have assumed that dependency is the opposite of independence. In fact, they are not contrary to each other, but are both mature qualities that complement a healthy way of being in the world. Wishing or pretending to grow out of the human condition of interdependency, or denying your vulnerabilities and needs for connections, would eventually be unsustainable.

If you can make peace with your need to depend on others for your progression in life, you will also recognize how much you have to offer. As others make their way into your world with their stories and yearnings, you can listen and offer your presence not out of a sense of superiority or perfection, but from a place of shared humanity.

If you have both been wounded before, in this place, you can each find your way back into connectedness via a gradual process in which you begin to feel safe enough to relax the self-protection, and to allow your vulnerabilities be seen, recognized and eventually accepted into the shared space. You can find a refuge in the other person while they find a sense of belonging in you. To this end, your awareness and willingness to stay open will allow you to create a space where mutual growth can take place. The most rewarding part of this journey is realizing that, rather than being preoccupied with a fear of exposing your vulnerabilities, you can now have relationships that are grounded in love and joy.

Once you have reconnected to your true nature, you will also remember how painful it is to block it. When you remove your armour, you will be able to have relationships that are open, congruent and mutually expressive. You will have the courage to be imperfect, to break through intellectualization and perfectionism, and you will no longer have to be seen as anything more than you are. You can openly self-disclose when it is appropriate. As you become more able to allow the intangible, unexpected and chaotic into your relationships, you also bring playfulness, humour, vitality and fun back into each encounter.

As you let go of old survival strategies and let in new light, focus on the limitless possibilities that are opening up. Slowly but surely, you can learn to express your true self in a safe environment, find a place in the world where you are celebrated rather than tolerated, and be grounded in peace rather than in fear. You can enter the chasm of change with the open heart of a mature adult. In this new place, you can trust without being overly rigid, or naively vulnerable, and love gloriously, generously and intelligently.

## Exercise: reconnecting with the feeling of love

The following exercise will help you to reconnect with a sense of open-heartedness towards others, as well as with your own empathic and compassionate self.

After reading through the instructions, you may wish to do this exercise with your eyes closed, and record it in your journal afterwards.

1  Start by bringing into your mind someone who makes you smile, whom you like or love dearly. It could be anyone: perhaps a mentor, a teacher that you admired, or even a pet. They do not have to be living.
2  Now imagine standing in front of that person, and he or she is smiling back at you.
3  As you think about your love and affection for this person, see if you can feel these emotions in your heart area. Try not to judge any feelings that arise as good or bad, right or wrong; as best you can, cherish and nourish whatever comes up for you.
4  Now imagine that the feelings of love and warmth are able to flow from you to the other person so that you can gently offer them to him or her.
5  Next, you may bring to mind all the people who love you and have loved you. Imagine all of them forming a circle that surrounds you. What do they wish for you? What do they see in you? Picture yourself receiving their love with a smile and a gentle bow, appreciating and absorbing their affection for you.
6  Now see if you can get in touch further with the feelings of love and softness in your heart area. Breathe in and out from that area, as if you are breathing from your heart.

7 Notice any other physical sensations and changes in your body – do you feel warm or cool? Are the muscles around your shoulders and forehead tight or relaxed? What else do you notice?

8 If you can visualize it, you may wish to imagine yourself as a blooming rose. As the petals slowly begin to open, you become aware that a blossoming is also occurring in the depth of your being. Something inside you is opening to the world, bringing warmth and beauty into the world.

The above imagery simply serves to reconnect you with the feelings of love and warmth within you. As the feelings arise, the specific details of the imagery do not matter. Recognize that these feelings are within you, independent of whether or not these people or objects are still with you, or what is happening in the outside world. You can call on these feelings simply by reconnecting with what is within you.

# Actualizing your creative potential

# Tapping into your creative vitality

Creative expression is what gives meaning to being highly sensitive and perceptively gifted.

Being a sensitive person by definition means you see what others don't see, and feel what others don't feel. Because of your multi-level awareness, there is more information that is available to you. You may have ideas that are not available to others and sometimes it even feels 'too much' – so much so that you wish you could put a stopper on the number and velocity of insights you get. This is where creativity comes in – it offers a safe outlet for your expression, insights and ideas.

The term 'creativity', like 'giftedness', has become a loaded term in modern society. Here, we are not equating creativity with publicly acclaimed achievements. You do not create meaning only when you call yourself an artist or a writer; you do so in the way you turn up every day to life and to work, or in the way you cook a meal, solve a conflict or have a good conversation.

Authentic expression is what gives us a sense of meaning in life. Sensitive and gifted people are prone to existential anxiety and depression: a constant feeling that there is something important they should be doing. Even when you are not certain what your mission is, or if it always seems out of reach, your search for it is constantly at the back of your mind. You experience this because you feel compelled to express whatever gifts you have; if you stifle them by hiding and shrinking, you are bound to feel restless and frustrated.

However, being imbued with visions and foresight does not always offer an easy path. Being truly creative means creating something that did not exist before. When we look at history, original contributions are often not appreciated at the time they are made. We only comprehend the magnificence of the work of artists such as Van Gogh after their deaths. As a natural shapeshifter, your task is to give people what they don't yet know they want. You are made not simply to fit into the world, but to bring new choices and insights into the world. Thus, honouring your path might mean that, for a while, others may misunderstand you, or reject what you have to say.

Inspite of its challenges, the creative path also brings extraordinary rewards. For the sensitive, gifted person, creativity starts with a sense of vitality that propels you to express your unique perspective and insights. When you follow your creative vitality, you have a focused vision that automatically weeds out doubts, confusion and decision-making fatigue. You will feel less restless, and less bothered by the inconveniences of daily life. Since you can no longer afford to procrastinate or be distracted, you also have no choice but to be courageous and assertive in saying 'no' to what doesn't serve you. Your purpose allows you to declutter your life, and to remove the physical and mental blockages that hold you back. As you continue along the path, you will eventually reach a point where your exhilaration will push any anxiety into the background. Before you know it, you have become a more resilient and productive version of yourself.

When you tap into your creative vitality, you also come to understand that it is your responsibility to use, rather than hide, your emotional gifts, sensitivity and perceptivity. Your ability to combine deep feelings with an active intellectual mind allows you to make a powerful contribution to the world. When you have a creative idea, you also have the responsibility of bringing it to fruition. Since there is only one of you, your expression is unique. If you block it, your expression will forever be lost to the world. Therefore, using your gifts is not an egotistical act but a responsibility. In making your mark, you create meaning not only for yourself but for the world, and you are not serving anyone by playing small.

## Exercise: tapping into your creative vitality

Find a quiet space, close your eyes and commit to giving yourself at least ten minutes. Now, let your mind wander and float back to a time when you felt a strong urge to express yourself.

You may be on your own or with others; you may be a child or an adult.

Perhaps you feel compelled to voice your opinion or to make something. You might have had the desire to express yourself in any shape or form: public speaking, writing, drawing, singing, or even holding a conversation.

However, we are not looking for a product, or an achievement, but simply a feel for your 'creative vitality', manifesting as an enthusiasm, an outburst of strong emotion, or a feeling of quickening that arises from within, which propels you to express your unique perspective and insights.

Set your inner critic aside. Look for nothing more than an urge, even if you did not move to action in the end.

If more than one memory emerges, choose one where you can most powerfully connect to, and clearly feel into, your own strengths. This is your creative vitality, the precious bridge between your natural gifts and your achievements in the world. Now, ask yourself:

✻ 'What do I believe about myself when I am in this state?'
✻ 'What do I believe about others and the world?'

Allow your creative vitality to seep into you; imagine it filling up your whole body.

You may sense it in your physical body as a warm glow that spreads through you, or see it as a light pouring down onto you. In whatever way works best for you, try and stay connected to the sensation for a few minutes without distractions.

# Looking inwards for your creative calling

Now that you can see part of your life's path as a sensitive person is to be a creative vessel, your next question might be: where do I start? Many people search for years trying to identify what they were meant to do, or who they were supposed to affect. Some describe it as a calling, others call it a voice, and often there is more than one answer. To not let the search for your calling become a daunting, overwhelming endeavour, you must realize that your creative calling does not come from something outside of you, but from within you.

In a world where the focus is always on what we produce, we can get lost letting what we make define who we are, rather than allowing our natural expression to flow through. The search for your calling, however, is an inside-out, rather than outside-in process.

There is a big difference between creating out of a need for social proof versus the pure joy of expressing oneself. When we do things out of a place of lack – lacking approval, recognition and applause – we become attached to the outcome. In contrast, when we set an intention to be nothing but the truest expression of who we are in this world, we are suddenly liberated from our egotistical fears.

Many successful artists and creators start out from a place of joy. They make things because they have a powerful need to express, and to be seen and heard for who they are. The process may start in a secret journal, in something they made in their bedroom, or in a childhood fantasy. However, when they get more attention from the world, many become enslaved by their creative success. This is when they start anxiously checking the feedback or comparing their success to that of others. As they attach more of their self-worth and self-definition with the outcome of their art, their world narrows down. Suddenly they live in a place where thoughts about work take up all the space and energy, everything feels personal, and all negative feedback seems like a personal attack. They desperately invest more and more into proving something to the world and end up in a vicious cycle where their life becomes devoid of joy. In the end, they squander the gift started their success in the first place.

Letting your work completely define you leaves you in an emotionally vulnerable position, where you become overly attached to praise and blame, gain and loss, and you run the danger of losing your integrity and forgetting what you value most. Conversely, focusing only on expressing your truest voice keeps you on track. As you get further into your creative flow state in this way, creativity becomes a process of continuously searching inwards. For the gifted and intense, the expression 'finding your voice' is not exactly accurate. Your task is actually to go in and 'remember' your voice. Your creativity is about owning, rather than denying, what you have always seen, felt and known. Think of it as a process of reverse-engineering, where you shed the layers of guilt and shame that have stopped you from expressing your astute observations, unique perspective on social dynamics, and revolutionary ideas that the world may not be ready to hear. Your unique creative contribution to the world radiates naturally out of your potential, your qualities and the essence of your being. Picasso rightly said that 'all children are artists'; however, our voices have been lost. Ask yourself: are you trying to make something happen – trying to work hard towards finding something that is not there – or are you merely expressing what is already there? Do you trust your basic goodness, your voice that is inside of you? If, whenever you feel stuck, you find the answer from within yourself, you will eventually come to trust what is already inside of you. Your life experience, your unique perspectives: these things will be lost if you do not bring them into the world with your voice. Your work then becomes exciting because you see yourself as a true creative powerhouse: a well so deep it can never be exhausted.

By owning your voice and showing up to the world as the sensitive empath that you are, you are championing not only your rights, but also those of all other passionate and intense people. Your courage will not only allow others to find refuge in your story, but you also liberate them to express their own.

Celebrating your gifts, and being unapologetically honest about your emotional reality as an intense person is not only personally healing, but also deeply meaningful.

### Exercise: looking inwards for your creative calling as a sensitive person

Your creative calling is not something that you search for outside of yourself, nor is it an external voice that you listen to. It is a gift that resides within you – all you need to do is to look inwards. Very likely, your soul has been trying to reach out to you through your actions, feelings and instincts. If you can only take some time to listen quietly, without any harsh judgement, it will guide you to the truth that brings you your answers.

Using the following questions as prompts, reflect in your journal:

1  **What captivates you in life?**
   Take a life inventory. Look at your long-term and childhood interests, and how you spend your free time. Review your bookshelf, your movie wish list, and any media content that you consume on a regular

basis. What most excites and energizes you? Whom do you admire, and why? Write down on a mindmap anything and everything you can think of that has inspired or influenced you: it may be a person, a book, a movie, a song, an article, a seminar, or even a memorable conversation.

2 **What makes your heart sing?**

What were your favourite things to do when you were a child? Make a list of the things that you do in your free time when nobody is watching. When does time seem to fly by? When you are engaged in activities related to something that makes your heart sing, you are likely to feel a profound sense of meaning, have excellent focus, or experience enormous energy. The process itself, rather than the outcome, rewards you.

3 **What makes your blood boil?**

What angers you, or frustrates you?

When was the last time you stood up for someone, or something? What was it about? Do you feel pain and frustration about the status quo of certain issues in the world? Do you see and feel what is lacking in a situation?

4 **What can you do that no one else can?**

Perhaps you have a vivid vision of how things could be different, or you have a unique idea of the potential of something.

Identify common themes in your list, and start narrowing them down to no more than three 'master' themes. Try not to censor or judge this process, or allow it to be limited by conventional wisdom. People's 'legacies' come in all shapes and forms: for some people it is about building a company; for others, it is about spreading an idea. Some wish to be the best parent they can be, while others want to express themselves authentically through art. You are also allowed to have more than one calling. The bottom line is, you can only strive be the best *you* can be: everyone else is taken.

# Being in creative alignment

Despite the bliss, joy and fulfilment that the creative process brings is not devoid of pain. Unlike many other types of work, its process is non-linear, intangible, unpredictable and – in a word – messy. You are used to moving forwards like a rocket, but on some days, you will have a creative 'dry spell'. Some call it writer's or artists' block, but you don't have to be in a traditional artistic endeavour to experience this. You know you are in a dry spell when you struggle to be creative despite your best efforts. Your creative angst may manifest as a lingering anxiety about not fulfilling your potential, a fear that you are 'wasting your life'. Many intense and gifted individuals struggle with the idea of `being' without `doing'. Because you can so clearly see what is possible, you almost feel obliged to work towards fulfilling your vision with every single minute you have. Even when this comes from a place of healthy drive towards excellence, it still manifests as a constant existential dread, a nagging feeling that somehow you have not worked hard enough, or been productive enough.

Perhaps you can remember a time when you excitedly embarked on a creative journey, feeling inspired and ready to achieve greatness. Then, a few months down the line, you were in an in-between zone that is chaos and uncertainty. This is when you are most likely to feel distraught, exhausted and confused. In fact, there is a term for this phenomenon, known as 'Kanter's Law' (Kanter, 1984): we are at our most vulnerable in the middle of our creative journey – away from the inspiring beginning and the exhilarating rush when we are close to the finish line. At this testing time, you can learn to draw strength from something greater than yourself. You have the opportunity to practise what I call 'creative alignment': a process of humbly leaning in and releasing some of your need to control. 'Creative alignment' is a buffer for your restlessness, despondency and fear: an essential skill you will want as you embark on your journey.

Being in creative alignment means you see yourself as nothing more than a vessel, or a conduit that channels creativity from a force larger than you. You do not need to be religious to find your alignment. Increasingly, successful artists and achievers around the world realize this wisdom. Elizabeth Gilbert (2009), the author of *Eat, Pray, Love* and *The Big Magic*, tells us that before the Renaissance, the idea of 'genius' was different from what it is now. The ancient Greeks and Romans believed that a person *has* a genius that works through them, rather than them *being* the genius. Close to our understanding of having a 'guardian angel', the Romans believed that a genius was a magical divine entity that would invisibly assist the artist with their work. With this view, you learn to see that whatever abilities and achievements you have are attributed to an unseen spirit, and you are not entirely on your own in giving birth to your creation. All you can do, then, is to show up and try your best, and the outcome is not up to you. Julia Cameron, author of the best-selling creativity guide *The Artist's Way* (1995), says, 'Life is a spiritual dance and that our unseen partner has steps to teach us if we allow ourselves to be led'.

We also find this wisdom in the sacred Hindu scripture *Bhagavad Gita* (Easwaran, 2007). In it, Krishna tells Arjuna that the right attitude is to focus on the integrity of the action without attachment to the outcome: 'Perform all thy actions with mind concentrated on the Divine, renouncing attachment and looking upon success and failure with an equal eye.' By focusing not on the praise and blame, but solely on expressing your truth, you will have the strength to persist in your chosen endeavour.

The practice of creative alignment is about balancing the tension between actions and receptivity. On a practical level, it involves actions such as maintaining your physical health, seeking advice from others, optimizing your energy and maximizing your creative output. On a more subtle and energetic level, these actions are balanced by your readiness to receive guidance and be open to input that is outside of your control. Once you have devoted full integrity to your work, you are free. As Woody Allen said, for artists, 'Eighty per cent of success is showing up.'

Learning about the inherent 'seasonal changes' in a creative process can also help you to be better equipped to ride the emotional waves during a creative tough patch. Any creative process has set phases. While the 'high' from producing tangible work is reassuring, it is not healthy or natural to always stay in that state. Imagine yourself as a gardener of your work [spaced en-rule] seeds need to be sown and watered before the plants can flourish. As well as time for actually generating words and images, you also need time for research, and for your ideas to take shape. This incubation phase can be difficult to bear if you do not have a sense of trust in the process.

You may have defined your creative output by the volume of work you complete, the time to give to others, the number of tasks you can tick on the checklist, or the sum of money you earn in a day. But often, more is operating in the background without you knowing. The time you take to rest, nap, play, take sabbaticals, and have fun can be just as productive (if not more so), and meaningful. Ironically, when we become attached to our rigid idea of what and how much we 'should do,' we sabotage the very thing that we are trying to achieve. Instead, we can be both at ease and creative by allowing our body's signals, curiosity and enthusiasm to guide us.

What if all the time that you spend 'indulging' in play, rest and pleasure are not a distraction from your work, but the springboard to it? Research has found that people who 'procrastinate' are more creative (Grant, 2017). This is because what we have previously condemned as 'procrastination' is actually a time of 'generative wander,' where we gather more information, and allow concepts to build and develop, eventually leading to more innovative ideas.

What if there was a wise internal mechanism built into you, operating in ways that your conscious mind cannot yet perceive? As all systems are designed to do, your subconscious mind is constantly working, adapting, adjusting, and making decisions to achieve a functional equilibrium. Like all things in nature, it yields to a natural rhythm that alternates between moving and stopping, generating and resting and, unless you resist it, it is completely in sync with how things 'should be'. I am not suggesting that you stop working altogether during a dry spell, but rather, recognize it for what it is, and make the best of it. The time when you are not actively producing can be an exciting time. It is the best time for you to return to the drawing board, to exercise your beginner's mind, to see everything with a fresh pair of eyes, and to ignite the child-like wonder in you. This is also a time when you can joyously forage in libraries and media to gather inspiration.

You are not generative ONLY when you are writing, drawing, acting, or working. You do not have to segregate your life's activities into the 'productive' or 'unproductive' camps, as they are all part of your creative life. In times when you go down the rabbit hole of blaming yourself for 'wasting time', or 'procrastinating,' see if you can think of these periods when you are flexing your creative muscles, not as an obstacle to your creative achievements, but as part of them. Trusting this subconscious natural order is infinitely more powerful than your conscious mind's planning, willing and judging.

Letting go and leaning into unseen forces is difficult for many gifted creative people, due to their propensity for constant striving and perfectionism. If this describes you, your first step may be to cultivate the trust that what is happening is 'enough'. You are not defined by what you make. You can tell yourself 'I am enough', then relinquish all need to justify your existence by being useful or productive. Your old, small, critical self may confuse letting go with laziness, but the wise part of you knows that constant pressure to do more and be more results in nothing more than chronic stress and anxiety and, eventually, burnout. Letting go comes from a place of love, while indolence comes from a place of fear.

You also lean in by seeing your quest for authentic expression as an ongoing, lifelong process. You were given your gifts, inspiration and passion because a source greater than you chose you to be a vessel of expression. Therefore, even if life doesn't follow the timeline you've drawn up, even when you are anxious about how slowly it is taking form, what will be done will get done. It is not your job to judge how fast you produce, how valuable your contribution is, nor how it compares with other people's work. All you need to do is to take one step after another and let life take care of the rest. If you are prone to being impatient, see if you can adopt a wider perspective. Your current step is simply one of many in your journey as a creative being, and your body's natural need for rest and rejuvenation is not a threat, but an ally, for the longer game. That way, you cease to be swayed by day-to-day fluctuations in your output.

At the heart of this practice is the mindset that your creative work is being done 'through you', rather than 'by you'. Leaning in is not about inaction. It's about taking action from a place of trust, and releasing our attachment to a particular outcome. Not only does this mindset take away stress and anxiety, it is also where your best work comes from. When you release your need to control, you open the door to receiving boundless energy, inspiration and peace. Even if pushing, striving and controlling have brought you success in the past, they may not be able to take you forward. Instead, try listening, trusting and allowing, and give yourself the opportunity to soak in the power of leaning in to creative alignment.

## Exercise: action and release

Use your journal for the following exercise.

1 Choose a topic or a creative project on which you feel stuck. It may be an issue in life where you feel stuck, an issue that you are struggleing to resolve, or a stagnant project that is sitting on your shelf.
2 Open your journal, lay it out flat in front of you, so you have available a blank double-page spread.
3 On the left-hand page write 'TO DO', and on the right-hand page write 'TO RELEASE'.
4 On the 'TO DO' page, make a list of all the actions that you can take to resolve the issue.
5 On the facing page, make a list of all the things that are beyond your control; these are the things that you can now choose to let go of, and surrender yourself to the natural order of life.

# A letter to passionate souls

If I were to sum up the message of this book in one sentence, it would be this: There is nothing wrong with you. Not only that, you are an extraordinary, unusually sensitive and courageous soul.

In our society, the norm is to try and cover up any intense emotion and existential anxiety through numbing. When things get too much, it is in our human nature to want to close our eyes and pretend that nothing is happening. Many people dull their wits through engaging in mindless activities or consuming short-lived pleasures. More often than not, passionless life is chosen because it feels, even if only superficially, easier and more secure.

However, those born with a sensitive and perceptive soul struggle to do that. Your sensitivity translates into a predisposition to feeling like a stranger in a strange land, to cry at the drop of a hat, to be wildly attuned to your surroundings and to be painfully empathic with those around you.

It is not that you try to be different, or pretend to be special, but that you simply cannot shut down your natural ability to see and feel so much. Perhaps you 'fail' to turn a blind eye to the harshness and darkness of reality, or to neglect our ultimate situations of death, change and uncertainty.

Your sensitivity makes it hard for you to fit into the hypocritical aspects of this world. You possess a particular kind of awareness of truth, injustice, suffering, and of painfully beautiful things. You may have been described as having a keen intelligence, and unbounded perceptivity; you may have been called, or may feel like, an old soul. Your sentimental nature means you are always pondering the transient nature of all things beautiful, and you are plagued by an intangible feeling of divine homesickness.

Even when others don't see it, and you have not yet recognized it, it actually takes a tremendous amount of courage to be you. Passionate engagement with life is not an easy road, and it is one less travelled. The word 'passion' is derived from the Latin verb *patio*, which means 'to suffer' and 'to endure'. Passionate living entails a kind of openness which means you are always engaging with the up and downs, gains and losses, and pleasures and pains in life. When you choose to walk the path of passion, you commit yourself to facing up to the bare bones of reality – including its embedded challenges and uncertainties, even when they hurt you, trouble you, and tire you out.

You may feel that you have no other option than to take life seriously, and you aspire to live fully and intensely, with complete presence and passion. Even when it is difficult, the intense and gifted soul inside you stubbornly refuses to be diluted. You want to embrace it all, with wide-open eyes. Deep down, you know that in the end, the joy and aliveness you will experience is in direct proportion to the suffering you can endure. In the end, without sensitivity what would life be? It is this part of you that has given your life so much colour and meaning. Although it is a source of both ecstasy and terror, it is also the source of all that is precious and memorable.

If you can elevate your level of thinking, you will see that being born into a world, a family, or a tribe as an extraordinarily sensitive, intense and gifted person is not an accident, nor is it unfortunate.

Perhaps you went through what you did in order to forge a new path. By no means would I want to diminish the pain of what you went through, but your experience is a portal to the discovery of your real purpose and destiny.

When you can allow yourself to examine your wounds and courageously revisit painful memories; when you can courageously and patiently allow your grief and anguish to do the work – without perpetuating or repressing them – you will eventually reach the depth of your psyche, where you will find the most profound growth and insights. As Leonard Cohen sang in his song 'Anthem': 'There is a crack in everything, that's how the light gets in'.

If you can be open to the possibility that everything you thought was 'wrong' is actually 'right', your world radically opens up. Suddenly, it all makes sense: your past experiences of being misunderstood and ridiculed are a part of life's invitation for you to come forward. Life is calling you to step up as a visionary, a passionate rebel, a gifted artist or a wise old soul. In this light, your struggles and sufferings are not meaningless, but an initiation.

Just like in a shamanic journey, you have been initiated into bringing passion and truth back into our collective psyche. By nature, you are the pioneers of the world: you are the questioners and progressives whose role is to shed light on the realities which others do not yet see or understand. You can deny it, fight it, but in the end, you will not be able to suppress your unique insights and perspectives. Although you might not have chosen this path, it is your path.

Your passion for life manifests as real gifts when you can combine it with your ability to see beauty and to make intellectual or creative connections. This is what artists and poets across history have done all their lives. Sadly, though, historically and up until today, those with visionary or insightful qualities are also deemed mad, pathological, or even schizophrenic by the world.

To channel your natural gifts into an artistic or productive output, you must first build a healthy relationship with your intensity. It is critical that you do not fall into the trap of regarding it as a disorder, or condition. Rather than being overwhelmed, oppressed and isolated by your sensitivity, you must use it to create structure and meaning, to find your tribe and, ultimately, to actualize your maximum potential.

Your sensitivity and intensity are the keys to your fullest potential. Hiding and shrinking prevent you from bringing your gifts into the world and you are not serving the world by playing small.

Once you have embraced your sensitivity, intensity and giftedness, you will realize that they are leading you to freedom and peace. You can finally stop fighting, trying to pretend to be who you are not, and suppressing and hiding your sensitive and intense nature. Living in authenticity is rich and full of paradoxes: groundless yet robust, frightening and reassuring, unfamiliar though it feels like home. In the unrest, you will feel an undercurrent of relief, excitement, hope and pleasure – waves of bliss, as if your deepest self has found its true home.

For now, I will leave you with this quote from *Demian: The Story of Emil Sinclair's Youth*, by Hermann Hesse (1919), and I wish you well on your utterly precious and heroic journey:

> 'We who bore the mark might well be considered by the rest of the world as strange, even as insane and dangerous. We had awoken, or were awakening, and we were striving for an ever perfect state of wakefulness...'

# Further reading

Adamski, A., 'Archetypes and the collective unconscious of Carl G. Jung in the light of quantum psychology', *NeuroQuantology*, 9 (3) (2011, pp. 563–71)

Ainsworth, M.D.S., Blehar, M.C., Waters, E. and Wall, S.N., *Patterns of Attachment: A Psychological Study of the Strange Situation* (Psychology Press, 2015)

American Mensa Ltd., 'Gifted characteristics', at: https://www.us.mensa.org/learn/gifted-youth/insights-into-gifted-youth/gifted-characteristics/ [Accessed 31 May 2017]

Andersen, H.C., *The Ugly Duckling* (IE Clark Publications, 1995)

Aron, E., *The Highly Sensitive Person* (Kensington Publishing Corp., 1996)

Aron, E., *The Highly Sensitive Person In Love: Understanding And Managing Relationships When The World Overwhelms You* (Harmony, 2001)

Aron, E., 'Is sensitivity the same as being gifted?' Comfort Zone email newsletter, November 2004 (www.hsperson.com)

Batson, C.D., 'Prosocial motivation: is it ever truly altruistic?', *Advances in Experimental Social Psychology*, 20 (1987, pp. 65–122)

Bernstein, G., *Spirit Junkie: A Radical Road to Discovering Self-love and Miracles* (Hay House, Inc., 2011)

Besel, L.D. and Yuille, J.C., 'Individual differences in empathy: The role of facial expression recognition', *Personality and Individual Differences*, 49 (2) (2010, pp. 107–12)

Bockian, N.R. and Villagran, N.E., *New Hope for People with Borderline Personality Disorder: Your Friendly, Authoritative Guide to the Latest in Traditional and Complementary Solutions* (Harmony, 2011)

Bowlby, J., *A Secure Base: Clinical Applications of Attachment Theory*, Vol. 393 (Taylor and Francis, 2005)

Bowlby, J., Robertson, J. and Rosenbluth, D., 'A Two-Year-Old Goes to Hospital', *The Psychoanalytic Study of the Child*, 7(1), (1952, pp.82–94)

Breathnach, S.B., *Simple Abundance: A Daybook of Comfort and Joy* (Hachette UK, 2011)

Brown, B., *The Power of Vulnerability: Teachings on authenticity, connection and courage* (Sounds True, 2012)

Cain, S., *Quiet: The Power of Introverts in a World that Can't Stop Talking* (Broadway Books, 2013)

Cameron, J., *The Artist's Way: A Course in Discovering and Recovering Your Creative Self* (Pan Macmillan, 1995)

Chikovani, G., Babuadze, L., Iashvili, N., Gvalia, T. and Surguladze, S., 'Empathy costs: negative emotional bias in high empathizers', *Psychiatry Research*, 229 (1) (2015, pp. 340–6)

Chodron, P., *Taking the Leap: Freeing Ourselves from Old Habits and Fears* (Shambhala Publications, 2009)

Clark, G.A. and Zimmerman, E., *Issues and Practices Related to Identification of Gifted and Talented Students in the Visual Arts* (No. 9202) (National Research Center on the Gifted and Talented, 1992)

Coelho, P., *Like the Flowing River: Thoughts and Reflections* (Harper Collins UK, 2006)

Cooper, J.F., *The American Democrat: Or, Hints on the Social and Civic Relations of the United States of America* (H. & E. Phinney, 1838)

Csíkszentmihályi, M., *Flow and the Psychology of Discovery and Invention* (New York: Harper Collins, 1996)

Csíkszentmihályi, M., *Flow, The Secret to Happiness* (TED Talk, 2004) at www.ted.com/talks/mihaly_csikszentmihalyi_on_flow

Curtis, H., *Everyday Life and the Unconscious Mind: An Introduction to Psychoanalytic Concepts* (Karnac Books, 2015)

Dąbrowski, K., 'The theory of positive disintegration', *International Journal of Psychiatry*, 2 (2) (1966, pp. 229–49)

Damasio, A.R., *Descartes' Error* (Random House, 2006)

Daniels, S. and Piechowski, M.M., *Living with Intensity: Understanding the Sensitivity, Excitability, and Emotional Development of Gifted Children, Adolescents, and Adults* (Great Potential Press, Inc., 2009)

Davis, M.H., 'Measuring individual differences in empathy: evidence for a multidimensional approach', *Journal of Personality and Social Psychology*, 44 (1) (1983, pp. 113–26)

Domes, G., Schulze, L. and Herpertz, S.C., 'Emotion recognition in borderline personality disorder – a review of the literature', *Journal of Personality Disorders*, 23 (1) (2009, pp. 6–19)

Dweck, C.S., *Mindset: The New Psychology of Success* (Random House Digital, 2008)

Easwaran, E., *The Bhagavad Gita* (Classics of Indian Spirituality) (Nilgiri Press, 2007)

Eisenberg, N. and Miller, P.A., 'The relation of empathy to prosocial and related behaviors', *Psychological Bulletin*, 101 (1) (1987, p. 91)

Eisenberg, N., Fabes, R.A., Miller, P.A., Fultz, J., Shell, R., Mathy, R.M. and Reno, R.R., 'Relation of sympathy and personal distress to prosocial behavior: a multimethod study, *Journal of Personality and Social Psychology*, 57 (1) (1989, p. 55)

Falk, R. F., Lind, S., Miller, N.B., Piechowski, M.M. and Silverman, L.K., 'The Over-Excitability Questionnaire – Two (OEQII): Manual, Scoring System, and Questionnaire', *Institute for the Study of Advanced* Development (Denver, 1999)

Fertuck, E.A., Jekal, A., Song, I., Wyman, B., Morris, M.C., Wilson, S.T., Brodsky, B.S. and Stanley, B., 'Enhanced "reading the mind in the eyes" in borderline personality disorder compared to healthy controls', *Psychological Medicine*, 39 (12) (2009, pp. 1979–88)

Fonagy, P., Luyten, P. and Strathearn, L., 'Borderline personality disorder, mentalization, and the neurobiology of attachment', *Infant Mental Health Journal*, 32 (1) (2011, pp. 47–69)

Franzen, N., Hagenhoff, M., Baer, N., Schmidt, A., Mier, D., Sammer, G., Gallhofer, B., Kirsch, P. and Lis, S., 'Superior "theory of mind" in Borderline personality disorder: an analysis of interaction behavior in a virtual trust game', *Psychiatry Research*, 187 (1) (2011, pp. 224–33)

Freed, J.N., 'Tutoring techniques for the gifted', *Understanding our Gifted*, 2 (6) (1990, p. 1)

Fromm, E., *The Art of Loving* (NY: Harper, 1956)

Gagné, F., 'Giftedness and talent: re-examining a re-examination of the definitions', *Gifted Child Quarterly*, 29 (3) (1985, pp. 103–12)

Gardner, H., *Frames of Mind. The Theory* (1983)

Gardner, H., ' "Multiple intelligences" as a catalyst', *The English Journal*, 84 (8) (1995, pp. 16–18)

Gardner, H., *Intelligence Reframed: Multiple intelligences for the 21st century* (Basic Books, 1999)

Gilbert, E., *Your Elusive Creative Genius* (TED Talk, February 2009), at: www.ted.com/talks/elizabeth_gilbert_on_genius

Gleichgerrcht, E. and Decety, J., 'Empathy in clinical practice: how individual dispositions, gender, and experience moderate empathic concern, burnout, and emotional distress in physicians', *PLoS One*, 8 (4) (2013, p. e61526)

Grandpierre, A., 'On the origin of solar cycle periodicity', *Astrophysics and Space Science*, 243 (2) (1996, pp. 393–400)

Grant, A., *Originals: How non-conformists move the world* (Penguin, 2017)

Hartmann, E., 'Boundaries of dreams, boundaries of dreamers: thin and thick boundaries as a new personality measure', *Psychiatric Journal of the University of Ottawa* (1989)

Hartmann, E., *Boundaries in the Mind: A New Psychology of Personality* (Basic Books, 1991)

Hartmann, E., 'The concept of boundaries in counselling and psychotherapy', *British Journal of Guidance and Counselling*, 25 (2) (1997, pp. 147–62)

Heidegger, M., *Ontologie: (Hermeneutik der Faktizität)*, Vol. 63 (Vittorio Klostermann, 1995)

Heidegger, M., *Being and Time: A translation of Sein und Zeit* (Suny Press, 1996)

Heller, L. and LaPierre, A., *Healing Developmental Trauma: How Early Trauma Affects Self-regulation, Self-image, and the Capacity for Relationship* (North Atlantic Books, 2012)

Hesse, H., *Demian: The Story of Emil Sinclair's Youth* (1919; trans. by Michael Roloff and Michael Lebeck, 1965)

Hoffman, E., *Vision of Innocence: Spiritual and inspirational experiences of childhood* (Boston: Shambala, 1992)

Jacobsen, M.E., *The Gifted Adult: A Revolutionary Guide for Liberating Everyday Genius* (Ballantine Books, 2000)

Jawer, M.A., 'Environmental sensitivity: inquiry into a possible link with apparitional experience', *Journal of the Society for Psychical Research*, 70 (882) (2006, pp. 25–47)

Jawer, M.A. and Micozzi, M.S., *Your Emotional Type: Key to the Therapies That Will Work for You* (Inner Traditions/Bear and Co., 2011)

Jeffers, S.J., *Feel the Fear and Do It Anyway* (Random House, 2012)

Jobs, S., Commencement Address (presented at Stanford University, 2005) at https://news.stanford.edu/2005/06/14/jobs-061505/

Jung, C.G., 'The fight with the shadow', *Listener*, 7 (7) (1946)

Kabat-Zinn, J., *Wherever You Go, There You Are: Mindfulness Meditation in Everyday Life* (Hachette UK, 2009)

Kanter, R.M., *Change Masters* (Simon and Schuster, 1984)

Kerns, K.A., Abraham, M.M., Schlegelmilch, A. and Morgan, T.A., 'Mother–child attachment in later middle childhood: assessment approaches and associations with mood and emotion regulation', *Attachment and Human Development*, 9 (1) (2007, pp. 33–53)

King Jr, M.L., 'Loving your enemies', *The Papers of Martin Luther King, Jr*, 4 (1957, pp. 315–24)

King Jr, D.M.L., Distinguished Service Award (Washington State University, 1995)

Klein, M., *Envy and Gratitude and Other Works 1946–1963* (London: The Hogarth Press, 1984)

Koelega, H.S., 'Extraversion and vigilance performance: 30 years of inconsistencies', *Psychological Bulletin*, 112 (2) (1992, p. 239)

Kohut, H., *The Restoration of the Self* (University of Chicago Press, 2009)

Kotler, S., *The Rise of Superman: Decoding the Science of Ultimate Human Performance* (Houghton Mifflin Harcourt, 2014)

Krippner, S., Wickramasekera, I., Wickramasekera, J. and Winstead, C.W., 'The Ramtha Phenomenon: psychological, phenomenological, and geomagnetic data', *Journal of the American Society for Psychical Research*, 92 (1) (1998, pp. 1–24)

Lawrence, D.H., *Studies in Classic American Literature*, Vol. 2 (Thomas Seltzer, 1923)

Lindberg, B. and Kaill, K.M., *Life Experiences of Gifted Adolescents in Sweden* (2012)

Livy, *The History of Rome*, Vol. 2 (Hackett Publishing, 1884)

Lovecky, D.V., 'Spiritual sensitivity in gifted children', *Roeper Review*, 20 (3) (1998, pp. 178–83)

McLaren, K., *The Art of Empathy* (Sounds True, Incorporated, 2013)

Melander, E.A., 'Effluvia and Aporia' (MFA Exhibition, Brigham Young University, 2012).

Miller, A., *The Drama of Being a Child: The Search for the True Self* (Virago, 1995)

Miller, A., *Breaking Down the Wall of Silence: The Liberating Experience of Facing Painful Truth* (Basic Books, 2008)

Millon, T. and Radovanov, J., 'Passive-aggressive (negativistic) personality disorder', in W. J. Livesley (ed.), *The DSM-IV Personality Disorders* (New York: Guildford Press, 1995, pp.312–25)

Minuchin, S., Baker, L., Rosman, B.L., Liebman, R., Milman, L. and Todd, T.C., 'A conceptual model of psychosomatic illness in children: family organization and family therapy', *Archives of General Psychiatry*, 32 (8) (1975, pp. 1031–8)

New, A.S., Rot, M.A.H., Ripoll, L.H., Perez-Rodriguez, M.M., Lazarus, S., Zipursky, E., Weinstein, S.R., Koenigsberg, H.W., Hazlett, E.A., Goodman, M. and Siever, L.J., 'Empathy and alexithymia in borderline personality disorder: clinical and laboratory measures', *Journal of Personality Disorders*, 26 (5) (2012, pp. 660–75)

Ogden, T.H., 'On projective identification', *The International Journal of Psycho-analysis*, 60 (1979, p. 357)

Olson, J., *The Slight Edge* (Greenleaf Book Group, 2013)

O'Neill, M., Calder, A. and Allen, B., 'Tall poppies: bullying behaviors faced by Australian high-performance school-age athletes', *Journal of School Violence*, 13 (2) (2014, pp. 210–27)

Orloff, J., *The Empath's Survival Guide: Life Strategies for Sensitive People* (Sounds True, 2017)

Park, L.C., Imboden, J.B., Park, T.J., Hulse, S.H. and Unger, H.T., *Giftedness and Psychological Abuse in BPD* (1992)

Piechowski, M.M., *Theory of Levels of Emotional Development* (Oceanside, NY: Dabor Science Publications, 1977)

Piechowski, M.M., 'Emotional giftedness: the measure of intrapersonal intelligence', *Handbook of Gifted Education*, 2 (1997, pp. 366–81)

Piechowski, M.M., 'Childhood spirituality', *Journal of Transpersonal Psychology*, 33 (1) (2001, pp. 1–15)

Piechowski, M.M., *Mellow Out, They Say. If Only I Could. Intensities and Sensitivities of the Young and Bright* (Yunasa Books, 2006)

Piechowski, M.M. and Colangelo, N., 'Developmental potential of the gifted', *Gifted Child Quarterly*, 28 (2) (1984, pp. 80–8)

Richo, D., *Daring to Trust: Opening Ourselves to Real Love and Intimacy* (Shambhala Publications, 2011)

Robinson, E., *The Original Vision: A study of the religious experience of childhood* (New York: Seabird Press,1983)

Roeper, A., 'How the gifted cope with their emotions', *Roeper Review*, 5 (2) (1982, pp. 21–4)

Roeper, A., *The 'I' of the Beholder: A Guided Journey to the Essence of a Child* (Great Potential Press, Inc., 2007)

St Maarten, A., *Divine Living: The Essential Guide To Your True Destiny* (Indigo House, 2012)

Sandemose, A., *A Fugitive Crosses his Tracks* (AA Knopf, 1933)

Shapiro, F., 'EMDR, adaptive information processing, and case conceptualization', *Journal of EMDR Practice and Research*, 1 (2) (2007, pp. 68–87)

Shilkret, R. and Nigrosh, E.E., 'Assessing students' plans for college', *Journal of Counseling Psychology*, 44 (2) (1997, p. 222)

Silver, T., *Outrageous Openness: Letting the Divine Take the Lead* (Simon and Schuster, 2016)

Silverman, L.K., *Counseling the Gifted and Talented* (Denver: Love Publishing Co., 1993)

Tronick, E., 'Still Face Experiment' (1975) at https://www.youtube.com/watch?v=apzXGEbZht0

Trotter, S.R., 'Breaking the Law of Jante', *Myth and Nation*, 23 (2015)

Tschann, Jeanne M., *et al.*, 'Resilience and vulnerability among preschool children: family functioning, temperament, and behavior problems', *Journal of the American Academy of Child and Adolescent Psychiatry*, 35.2 (1996, pp. 184–92)

Williamson, M., *A Return to Love* (New York: HarperCollins, 1992, p. 165)

Williamson, M., *A Woman's Worth* (Random House Digital, 1993)

Winnicott, D.W., 'The theory of the parent-infant relationship', *The International Journal of Psycho-Analysis*, 41 (1960, p. 585)

Young, J.E., Klosko, J.S. and Weishaar, M.E., *Schema Therapy: A Practitioner's Guide* (Guilford Press, 2003)

Zanarini, M.C., Williams, A.A., Lewis, R.E. and Reich, R.B., 'Reported pathological childhood experiences associated with the development of borderline personality disorder', *The American Journal of Psychiatry*, 154 (8) (1997, p. 1101)

# Index

sadness, 129
  acknowledging, 87, 96–7, 98–9
safe place visualization, 119
safety
  feeling of, 116–20
  in self-expression, 157–61
Sandermose, Aksel, 67
scapegoating, 6, 54–6
*Schadenfreude*, 168–9
schema reinforcement, 115–16
secure base, 117–20
self-awareness, 29, 145–8, 163
self-criticism, 59, 77, 130–3
self-esteem, 58
self-expression, 156–61
self-healing, 125–6
self-preservation, 70–1, 112–16,
  202–6
self-reflection, 7
senses, heightened, 5, 12, 21, 36
sensitivity to others' emotions *see*
  empathy
sensual over-excitability (OE), 36
separation anxiety, 72, 203
Shadow, 180–4
shame, feelings of, 44–5, 76–9
  letting go, 87
sharing experiences, 93–4, 158–60
Shilkret, R. and Nigrosh, E. E., 72
'should' and 'shouldn't' beliefs, 154–5
Silver, Tosha, 139
social anxiety, 76
spiritual giftedness, 31–2
spiritualism, 7
  trust in life's flow, 137–40
St Maarten, Anthon, 156
standing out, 64
  envy from others, 65–8
  hiding and shrinking, 68–74
Still Face Experiment (Tronick), 56

stimulation management, 14–15, 129,
  198, 199–200
stress
  chronic, 199
  hormone (cortisol), 58
survivor guilt, 72–3

talent vs. giftedness, 26–7
Tall Poppy Syndrome, 65, 66
thyroid problems, 199
toxic relationships, 166–79, 194–7
tranquility, 142–3
transference, 186–92
triggers, 82–4, 101
  time spent with family, 104–5
Tronick, Edward, 56
trust
  in life's flow, 137–40
  in others, 93–4, 118, 158–60
truth
  about yourself, 142–50, 152–5,
  161–3
pointing out, 156

*Ugly Duckling, The* (Andersen), 71, 144
ulcers, 19
unbalanced relationships, 195–6
under-stimulation, 129, 198, 199–200
unmet needs, 193

virtues, 155, 183
visualization exercise, 119
vulnerabilities, 51, 204–5, 208

Williamson, Marianne, 73, 147
women, hiding and shrinking, 73

Young, Jeffrey, 85
Young, Margaret, 162